John E. Land

Columbus: Her Trade, Commerce and Industries 1892-1893

Manufacturing Advantages, Business and Transportation Facilities

John E. Land

Columbus: Her Trade, Commerce and Industries 1892-1893
Manufacturing Advantages, Business and Transportation Facilities

ISBN/EAN: 9783743395350

Manufactured in Europe, USA, Canada, Australia, Japa

Cover: Foto ©Suzi / pixelio.de

Manufactured and distributed by brebook publishing software (www.brebook.com)

John E. Land

Columbus: Her Trade, Commerce and Industries 1892-1893

PUBLISHERS' NOTICE.

The labor connected with such a work as this none can fully appreciate but those who have performed it. The work is presented to the public with the belief that it is as nearly accurate as such works can be. The utmost care has been exercised in the collation and presentation of the matter in this work, especially that relating to the manufacturing and commercial advantages of Columbus, and no expense has been spared to make it not only acceptable to the general reader, but in the highest degree valuable to our tradesmen, manufacturers and financial institutions. The book is mainly designed to furnish the most comprehensive and authentic information concerning the facilities and resources of this city, which will awaken a more appreciative spirit of enterprise at home, and increase patronage and favor from abroad. It also aims to direct attention to our vast capabilities and resources, many of which are yet undeveloped, and to utilize more thoroughly the facts which demonstrate the superiority of Columbus as a commercial and manufacturing city. In a city like Columbus, where improvement and change are the order, and the watchword, it would be strange, indeed, if we did not here and there find an error. If, however, our pen shall succeed in directing the attention of the trade to its manifold superiorities, or draw to this vicinage a population that shall sieze upon its possibilities and go forward to glad fruition—controlling its agencies and shaping its destinies; if we do all or any of these, we shall be munificiently rewarded, and our chiefest aim be reached.

It remains for us now to acknowledge obligations to the various sources from which we have received assistance. Our object, throughout, having been to produce a useful book, we have not felt at liberty to reject aught that could be turned to practical use. Therefore, as far as was consistent with our own plan, we have carefully gleaned whatever was pertinent and of value we have discovered in other directions. Nor have the newspapers been overlooked. To the Directors of the Columbus Board of Trade, for their indorsement and hearty co-operation; to A. G. Grant, for the excellent photographs from which the cuts were made, and to the patrons of the work, who compose so valuable a portion of the business men, and are contributing most largely to the growth and prosperity of Columbus, the publishers desire to return their grateful acknowledgements.

With this brief preface, we launch our vessel, trusting that it may bring to port the treasures which the merchants and business men of the Queen City so richly deserve.

Very truly,

July 15, 1892. THE PUBLISHERS.

STATISTICS AND INDUSTRIES OF COLUMBUS.

The Columbus Board of Trade,
Columbus, Ga., February 29, 1892.

We, the undersigned, Directors of the Columbus Board of Trade, have examined a prospectus and plans submitted by the J. E. Land Publishing Co., of Chicago, contemplating the publication of a book setting forth the advantages and industries of Columbus, Ga., for general circulation, and take pleasure in recommending the enterprise for a favorable consideration of the business men of Columbus. It has been the desire of the Board of Trade, and the Committee on Statistics and Advertising, to publish such a work, and we think the proposition of the J. E. Land Publishing Co. offers the best inducements for a publication of that kind.

Respectfully,

L. H. CHAPPELL, President.
W. C. BRADLEY, 1st Vice-President.
WILLIAM A. WIMBISH, 2d Vice-President.
L. C. FRAZER, 3d Vice-President.
J. J. MOBLEY.

THOS. GILBERT, PRINTER, COLUMBUS, GA.

GENERAL INDEX.

A

B

C

D

E

F

G

H

I

J

K

L

M

V

W

Y

CORRECTIONS.

Since putting the article of the Chattahoochee Brewing Company in type, Mr. H. H. Epping, jr., has been elected President, *vice* E. H. Epping.

In the article of M. Seligman, page 75, the location should read 22 Tenth St.

Page 124—The firm of Hill, Reese & Co. changed to Geo. Reese & Co., office over R. Jefferson, cor. Broad and Eleventh streets.

Page 136—E. M. Averett—Location of business house 945 Broad street.

COLUMBUS, GA.:

THE QUEEN CITY OF THE SOUTH.

INTRODUCTORY.

FREEDOM of industry, the printing press, steam and electricity, neither of which were enjoyed in ancient times, are the four grand forces in the economy of modern times, which renders our civilization higher than that enjoyed by the ancients—the day-star of mankind, the solar-light of the human race.

The ancients were largely devoted to war; only a select few to literature, mainly in its less utilitarian departments. The industrial arts found no appreciable place in their systems, and material development was regarded important only so far as it was necessary to national defense or aggressive military operations. In modern times, on the other hand, the interests of industry—agriculture, manufactures and commerce—all the useful arts and avocations have been exalted to the first importance; all other considerations are made subordinate to these. If any proof were needed of the transcendent importance of industrial development to human progress, what more forcible, what more eloquent testimony could be required than is afforded by the record modern civilization has made in the last three or four centuries, contrasted with the record of fifty odd centuries of earlier times? Unquestionably it is to industrial development that civilization must look for a realization of its highest hopes. "For it is to be remembered," says Wells, "that the material needs of man must first and always be fairly satisfied before morality, certainly, in any high degree, is likely to exist among the masses; and furthermore, that something of material abundance or wealth must be earned and saved before leisure for study can be obtained, or the scholar can exist." But to supply the "material needs" of man begets a diversity of employment—the producer, the dealer, the common carrier, the manufacturer, the merchant, the banker, the officers of the law, all the army of trades and professions entering into the machinery of society and forming a city. How senseless, then, and unworthy of Cicero, was his remark: "Commerce is a sordid affair when it is of little consequence; for the small traders cannot gain without lying: it is a business only tolerable at best, when carried on on a large scale, and in order to supply the country with provision." This only serves to show how little the true interests of society were studied, how little they were understood in his time. With such sentiments prevailing, it is not to be wondered at that so little progress was made in *real* civilization during the long centuries of antiquity.

Striking as is the contrast between the progress made in ancient times and

RESIDENCE OF JOS. K. LAMB, EAST HIGHLANDS.

that made by modern civilization, the contrast between the progress of modern nations of Europe and that of the people of this country is hardly less remarkable. Scarcely more than a century has elapsed since the dawn of our national existence, at which period nine-tenths of the vast country we now occupy was an unexplored wilderness. Yet, in that comparatively brief time we have grown to be one of the greatest, and in many respects *the greatest* of the nations of the earth. From a population of 3,000,000, we have reached over 60,000,000 greater than any nation in Europe fully civilized, and greater than any on the globe except China, India and Russia. During this period we have increased in population more than 1700 per cent., while the nations of Europe, as a whole have increased less than 75 per cent. In area but two nations surpass us—Russia and China while in other physical conditions ours is incomparably superior to either. We lead all other nations in national wealth. In the value of manufactured products, of agriculture, of the carrying business, or transportation, and of mining, we are in advance of any other country: and in the six leading lines of business or pursuits, including the above, and also commerce and banking, taken as a whole, no nation equals ours. While we are, perhaps, the wealthiest nation on earth, our public debt at the same time is incomparably less than any of the more important nations. Of telegraph lines we have twice as many miles as any other people, and of railroads, more than all Europe, and half as many as the entire world. Cities are said to be the product of ages: yet, young as our country is, we are already third among the nations in respect to important cities. Speaking of the wonderful progress of this country, a writer in a recent number of the *Edinburg Review* says:

"Very naturally, our American friends are in the habit of boasting of the colossal scale of everything in their magnificent continent. Their lakes are seas, and their rivers are navigable for many thousand miles above the mighty estuaries. The very parks which are locked away within the recesses of their grand mountain ranges, might pass for provinces or principalities in the cramped countries of the Old World. Yet, engineering science, backed by unlimited capital, has overcome these formidable obstacles and barriers, flinging bridges everywhere across broad rivers, and carrying railroads by every gradient through the passes of the mountain chasms: everywhere they may point with legitimate pride to the triumphs of mind and energy over matter. Agriculture has kept pace with manufacturing industry, while it has far out-stripped commerce. The boundless prairies are being reclaimed by indefatigable labor, and the buffalo and roving savage have given place to herds of sleek cattle with their stockmen. Mining has made greater millionaires than manufactures: discoveries of minerals and of mineral oils have directed the rush of immigration to the most savage districts of the continent, till, from the Golden Gate of San Francisco to the quays of New York, and from the shores of Lake Superior to the mouth of the Mississippi, the States are being settled up by a community that is being steadily consolidated by the spread of a vast net-work of railway lines. Clusters of wooden shanties shoot up into towns, while towns that are favored by situation or circumstances, grow rapidly into great cities: nor is there any surer road from competence to wealth than judicious investment in eligible building lots."

With the record of such triumphs as we have pointed out, achieved in so short a time, who will attempt to picture the future of this magnificent country? Does any one doubt that it is capable of supporting a population as dense as Great Britain? Yet, settled as thickly as those islands it would contain a billion inhabitants—three times the present population of all Europe, and half that of the entire globe. If to-day, with sixty million inhabitants, this is the greatest industrial nation under the sun, when the resources of the country are but little more than explored, to what degree of grandeur and splendor may we not justly expect it to attain in the future? It is not surprising that the marvelous progress of the country has attracted the wonder and admiration of the civilized world; but when it is considered that this progress is, in a great measure, due to the Southern States—to the "Sunny South," as they have been appropriately called what must be thought of the magnificent resources of this new empire of material wealth and of the splendid enterprise of the people to whom its destiny has been committed.

ENTRANCE TO BOULEVARD, NORTH HIGHLAND.

If modern civilization has so much surpassed the "splendid barbarians" of antiquity in every department of human progress: if in this country we so transcend the people of Europe in every ratio of material advancement: if the "New South" has sounded the bugle-call and leads the onward march of business and industrial development, can it be regarded as more than every economic condition suggests to say that in this sunny clime, this great dominion, as boundless in material resources and in the enterprise of its multiplying millions as in its area, a queen-like metropolis will stand, a splendid monument of civic grandeur and magnificence? To ask the question is to answer it; for nature made the decree, so that he who runs may read, that here in Georgia, on the banks of the Chattahoochee river, is located the city to which all streams of traffic, and the industries of learning and the liberal arts will flow. With the discernment to see this, and the energy to anticipate it, Columbus will make herself the crowning scene of this great human sea, and through the vista of approaching years we behold the *Metropolis of the "New South.*"

EMBRYONIC COLUMBUS.

But before passing to the present condition of our City's trade, we deem it appropriate to give some brief account of its past condition, the better to show her importance, and the claims she has upon the country. All civilization grows up from, and out of, small centers and humble resources. A man, a house, a village and a machine, are the starting points of new and grand developments of commercial success, social life and national history. The world is full of such records, that find illustration and culmination in the fame, and wealth and power that gives success and triumph to personal enterprise and stability and grandeur to a city's history. Columbus is rich in annals, rich in associations that make her plains historic, her hills remarkable, and her name beloved and honored in many a clime. "These, then, are the treasured memorials of her people." These, whether they come down from the dim and shadowy past, or have their birth and fruition in the near and still remembered, are the only antiquities of the place and of her citizens. In the usual acceptation of the term, our country has no antiquities. Art, science, literature, music, poetry, war, have left no records—given us no monuments. But its *physical condition* glorious, comprehensive phrase! taking in, as it were, in one grand respiration, its unapproachable climate, its areable fields, its clear, swift-rolling rivers, its unhidden and exhaustless mineral wealth, its unent forests—these are the monuments; and monumental, too, of the "Eternal Power and Godhead." Aside from these and with these, what do we lack, for aught that wisdom can employ, or skillful labor produce? Our only real antiquities are reminiscencies of Indian life and warfare, and a recital of the hardships, endurance and fortitude of pioneer struggles. The former, as to its origin and incidents, is involved in mystery and mixed with fable. But it is replete with interest to the curious, and gorgeous with thrilling tales of field and flood to the workers of fiction. The latter blushes yet in virgin loveliness and beauty, and yet lifts its maiden hands, emploring Old Mortality to decipher its inscriptions, to freshen its facts, to revivify its memories and hand down to the generations coming and to come, "the short and simple annals" of a people who, coming from their homes beyond the mountains and on the eastern shore, settled on the banks of the beautiful Chattahoochee, whose fertile valleys their children have enriched as a garden, and made to bloom and blossom as a rose.

Since that time years have rolled around: years of history, civil and social, personal and domestic, unfold their pages of trial and triumph, progress and pause, toil and suffering, virtue and vice, life and death. War, fire, famine and pestilence have held high carnival in her centre; and the march of youthful art, science, trade, commerce and literature approach, anxious to be chronicled; while festivals and feasts, religion and licentiousness, each "come trooping up like bannered armies," with their contributions of glory or of shame, to fill the measure of the city's history. The leaves are brimming full: the acts and incidents are innumerable. Would that we could open the long-closed volume and bring things long hidden out into the sunlight, make scenes long lying in obscurity, names long lost in the whirlpool of life, voices long silent, address us from the graves of the past: but such is not our task. Therefore, we shall only garland a few of the reminiscences, skip lightly over the remainder, and speak with words of soberness of the great and living present.

LAKE ANNIE, WILDWOOD PARK, EAST HIGHLANDS.

From the most authentic information relative to the condition of the country about Columbus at the time of its earliest settlement, we are led to believe that the hills were covered with cedar, its valleys and low places hid by a dense undergrowth of bushes, while the level country around about was "peopled" by dense forests of cotton-wood, oak, magnolias, and such other lordly giants of the vegetable kingdom. Turning our imagination back to those early times, we can but feel an inward sublimity of its early charms. On the bosom of the beautiful river that courses its valleys, we see the Indian's bark canoe: vast herds of elk and horse, "wild and untamed," roaming through its dusky wilds: the eagle, swift on its prey and bold in its flight, "on cliffs and cedar-tops its eyries build.

ing:" the timid deer, basking at will in the genial sunbeams; or the winding smoke laizily ascending from the wigwam by the river's margin: warrior and maiden, chief and brave, are here in glorious contentment, discussing in colloquial pleasure, brave deeds or simple loves in their home,

"Shut out by alpine hills from the rude world."

Standing there upon the hills opposite the city, what a grand and magnificent prospect would here unroll itself before our vision; the far-off hills that now skirt the city's suburbs, blackened by dense foliage: the broad surface of the river stirred to gentle rolling by the evening breeze, and dashing its silvery spray against the rocks of its rugged banks, the rolling, undulated surface of the soil: the tangled background of cliff and cloud empurpled by the brush of heaven: all would here make up a scene presenting a marvelous master-piece of an omnipotent artist, a landscape as sublime and imposing in its grandeur as the Yosemite Valley, which distinguished the brush of Bierstadt, and gave his name to the roll of immortality. No churlish plowshare had ever marred the velvet of the old mossy green sward: no cultivator's fire had ever rioted in the wild, luxuriant undergrowth that waved its graceful plumage in every sheltered dingle, or in the tufted clumps of cedar that flaunted their verdant banners on every knoll and hillock: no axe had ever razed the gnarled and knotty barks of the huge oaks, time-honored and immortal Titans, which, scattered far and near in their mighty grandeur, lifted their white, thunder-splintered heads, "stag-horned, and sear, and blasted," above their less pretentious neighbors. Beneath their shadow the bow-string of the dusky hunter twanged terror to the antlered monarchs of the forest. Perhaps they stood here in their youth, when the boom of Columbus' gun announced to the whole world that a new land had been found. We know they were here, proud in meridian majesty, when America's unconquered legions swept on, like a moving wall of brass, against the scarlet-coated mercenaries of the British lion. But lo! a change has come over these tranquil scenes: the forest has disappeared, and up from the productive soil has vegetation sprung: the briar patch has been turned into a cotton patch: deep into the hillside the emblems of agriculture have fastened their roots, and no more will the startled stag bound from his lair when the crack of the rifle is heard in the valley, for some daring hunter has looked down upon it from the bordering hills, and claimed it as the heritage of his children: the foot-prints of the Anglo-Saxon are made in its rich soil, and are impressed forever the age of civilization has begun.

Columbus was established as a trading town in 1827, by an act of the Georgia Legislature. Twelve hundred acres were allotted for the town and commons, and a reservation of ten acres square for the county buildings of Muscogee county, the county having the privilege of selling any portion not needed for county buildings.

The first sale of town lots, consisting of a half acre each, began on the 10th day of July, 1828, and closed on the 23d; out of 632 lots laid off, 488 were sold, the total proceeds of the sale being $130,991.

In 1828 the first manufacturing establishment was built, and consisted of a turning lathe, erected on a little branch north of the city. In the same year the first theatre was built, and opened in July with a very creditable performance.

NOKOMIS ROCK, NORTH HIGHLANDS PARK.

In 1828 the first bale of cotton ever sold in the town was brought in November from Gwinnett county. It was sold at 12½ cents per pound.

In November, 1828, the first boat landed at the wharf. It was called the "Rob Roy," and was owned by a man named Love. Her cargo consisted of groceries for J. Fontain, Maharrey, Love & Co.

In 1828 the town was incorporated by an act of the Legislature, but the bill was not signed until the 19th of December, and provided for an election to be held on the first Monday in January, 1829, for an Intendent and six Commissioners.

The first Mayor of the town of Columbus was Ulysses Lewis, who was elected January, 1829, and R. T. Marks was the first City Clerk.

The first ordinance passed by the city government was one requiring all houses on the public streets and common to be removed, and forbidding all persons to cut down or destroy any tree on the river common. In 1829 the first bank was organized, and was called the Bank of Columbus.

In 1828, the first newspaper was established by Marebeau B. Lamar, and was called the *Columbus Enquirer*. The first paper was issued in May of that year, it was a weekly paper, and was ably edited.

On the 14th of March, 1839, the first fire occurred in the city. The quotations for this year were: Cotton 8¼ to 8½; bagging 23; bacon 9 to 12½; coffee 15 to 17: sugar 10 to 12; flour $8 to $9; meal 75; molasses 45.

In 1831 a new bank was organized, called the Farmers Bank of Chattahoochee, with E. S. Shorter President, and Edward Carey Cashier.

The following shows the condition of the banks in 1832:

NAME	CAPITAL	CIRCUL'N	DEPOSITS	SILVER	GOLD
Bank of Columbus.............	$ 120,000	$ 229,972	$ 13,603 50	$ 132,951 92	$ 301 50
Farmers' Bank.................	60,000	91,881	32,579 00	70,171 71	18,000 00
The Insurance Bank.......... ..	150,000	101,299	7,965 23	70,375 73	....
Totals	$ 330,000	$ 423,152	$ 54,147 73	$ 273,499 35	$ 18,301 50

In 1836, there was considerable trouble with the Indians who inhabited the Alabama side of the river. There were a number of fights, and on one occasion they fired into a steamboat, and killed the pilot who was on duty at the time.

In 1836, the town of Columbus was incorporated as a city, and an election held January 2d for a Mayor and six Aldermen, with the following result: John Fontaine, Mayor; T. G. Gordan, Geo. W. Dillard, Hampton S. Smith, E. Sigourney Norton, Thos. C. Evans and Ernest L. Wittich as Aldermen.

In 1841, the bridge across the river was swept away by a freshet, but was rebuilt during the same year by John Godwin, at a cost of $15,000.

On March 15, 1842, the first big fire occurred in this city. The total loss was $100,000. One death, that of Prof. G. R. Hurlburt, occurred by the the explosion of Boswell & Billing's drug store. The origin of the fire was a mystery, and was never explained.

April 14, 1843, the first bank robbery was committed, when the Western Insurance and Trust Company was robbed of some $60,000. One Thomas McKeen was arrested and gave information as to where the money was hid. All but $6,000 was recovered.

In February, 1844, the total valuation of city property was $1,266,055.

In December, 1844, the *Times* gives the following list of establishments: "Dry goods stores, 26; groceries, 57; provisions, 23; silver smiths, 5; clothing, 5; hats and caps, 1; hardware, 2; books and stationery, 2; saddle and harness, 3; tobacconists, 1; shoes, 7; bar-rooms, 17; auction stores, 2; drugs, 5; crockery, 1; confectioner, 1; tinware, 2; cabinet warehouses, 4; bakeries, 3; cotton warehouses, 5; livery stables, 4; hotels, 4; book-binderies, 2; iron foundry, 1; printing offices, 3; bank and bank agencies, 4; blacksmiths, 10; carriage warehouses, 2; cotton gin maker, 1; wheelrights, 3. Total 209."

In 1845 the first cotton mill was erected. They had 1,200 spindles at work, but were making improvements every day.

In 1845, the price of cotton ranged in January at 2 to 4½c. The first bale of the new crop that year was sold August 5th, at 8¼c. The market for the new commercial year opened in September at 6¼@7c., and dropped to 5½@6½c. in November. The closing quotations, December 16th, were 5½@6½c. The receipts for the year ending August 31st, were about 85,000 bales, a decrease of 30,000 bales from the preceding year.

The first Board of Trade was organized July 3, 1845, with Henry King, Chairman, and C. E. Mims, Secretary.

In 1847, the city made a subscription to the Muscogee Railroad (now the Southwestern), and during this year there were numerous fires, but not so disastrous as in previous years, as the city fire companies were better able to cope with the fire fiend.

In 1848, the subscription to the Muscogee Railroad was ratified, and it was agreed at an election, by a vote of 337 to 27, that a special railroad tax for a town of two years, of 2 per cent. on real estate, and one-quarter of one per cent. on sales of merchandise and banking business, should be levied to meet the subscription.

The first telegraph line reached Columbus in July, 1848. In 1849-50 the city continued to grow, the factories already here enlarging their plants, while the building of the Muscogee Railroad was pushed forward with rapidity.

In 1851, the first agitation of a waterworks was begun, and the first agricultural fair was held in November of that year.

In 1852, the first gas company was formed. The city council appropriated $10,000 to the capital stock of the company.

In March, 1853, a severe storm swept over the city, doing considerable damage unroofing and otherwise damaging houses, blowing down chimneys, etc The damage done was estimated at from $50,000 to $100,000, but no lives were lost.

From 1853 to 1856 the city continued to grow, and notwithstanding the financial difficulties of 1855, subscribed and voted capital stock to two railroads.

In 1860, the United States census showed the population of Columbus to be —whites, 5,674; slaves, 3,265; free negroes, 100 -Total, 9,036. In this year political excitement ran high, and a number of military companies were organized.

In December, 1861, the first year of the war, we find the following market quotations: Bacon, 25 to 30c.: flour, $10 to $12: coffee, 67½c.; sugar, 10 to 12c.: salt, $10 per sack; corn, 85c. to $1: wheat, $2; prints 15 to 20c.

From 1861 to 1865, the city was at a stand-still—a natural result—caused by the war between the States. On April 16, 1865, the Federal forces under command of Gen. Wilson, succeeded in capturing the city, after a hotly contested fight by the few hastily organized troops, and the city was badly looted and many houses burned. After peace was declared, the energetic people of Columbus began a system of building up their lost fortunes and their city's greatness, and out of the ashes of the old Columbus has grown this magnificent city—"The Queen City of the South"—with the mammoth cotton factories, warehouses, etc., her palatial dry goods and grocery houses, and her magnificent residences.

At this juncture of our labors we may, with propriety, change the current of our remarks. We have brought the records of our city—in a rude and imperfect manner though it be—down to a period within the memory almost of even our youngest citizens. However, we by no means claim to be the historian of the city, and trenching in no part upon ground that properly belongs to the domain of biography, we have sought only to balance all drafts upon the Past by

WEROCOBA DRIVE, EAST HIGHLANDS.

the marvelously increased value of the Present, demonstrating the philosophy of political economy in the presentation of *cause* by the grander illustration of *effect*. Therefore, we may say the past of this city has been well cared for, and as a Neophyte in Archaeology, one may well, then, despair of success, and devote attention to the actual and THE PRESENT of our city, which, sustained by energy backed by capital, stimulated with fortitude by virtue of success, presents with its material progress, its advances in commerce and manufactures, its internal navigation by river and rail, its industrial features, its telegraphy, telephones, electric lights, its enlightened press, its metropolitan advancements in every particular, themes sufficiently comprehensive and voluminous, and to which we invite the closest attention, and in which we promise faithful account of its magnitude and development. In this connection we may say,

PROSPECTIVELY,

Her destiny is fixed: like a new-born empire she is moving forward to conscious greatness. In her bosom all the extremes of the country are represented, and to her growth all parts of the country contribute. Mighty as are the possibilities of her people, still mightier are the hopes inspired. The city that she now is, is only the germ of the city that she will be, with her hundreds of thousands of souls occupying her vast domain. Her strength will be wonderful, and as she grows toward maturity, her institutions of learning and philosophy will correspondingly advance. If we but look forward in imagination to her consummated destiny, how grand is the conception! We can realize that there will be built great halls and edifices for art and learning: here will be represented some future great teachers of religion, teaching the ideal and spiritual development of the race, and the higher allegiance of man to the angel-world: here will live some future Plutarch, who will weigh the great men of his age: here some future "Mozart will thrill the strings of a more perfect lyre, and improvise grandest melodies" for the congregated people: here some future "Rembrandt, through his own ideal imagination, will picture for himself more perfect panoramic scenes of nature's lovely landscapes." May we not justly rejoice in the anticipation of the future greatness of the civil, social, intellectual and moral elements which are destined to form a part of the Columbus of the future? and may we not realize that the thousands who are yet to be its inhabitants will be a wiser and better people than those of this generation, and who, in more perfect life, will walk these streets of the city of the future with softer tread, and sing music with sweeter tones, be urged on by aspirations of higher aims, rejoice with fuller hearts, and adorn in beauty, with more tender hands, the future Queen City of the South?

COLUMBUS AS IT IS IN 1892.

The entire length of the city shows a magnificent river frontage of more than three miles, forming a beautiful and picturesque curvature, while the thickly settled suburbs beyond give it even greater frontage. The average breadth of the city is two miles, and the greatest width two and two-thirds miles.

THE QUEEN CITY PROSPECTIVE.

From the more prominent points about the city, and particularly the hills across the river in Alabama, a fine view is obtained of the city and the surrounding country, which, lying like a vast amphitheatre, the range of hills forming the segment of a circle, and stretching far away to the North and South, about three miles equi-distant from its central point, makes up a picture of hill and dale, ravine and river, city and country, exceedingly grand and lovely. The beautiful suburban towns, and the thickly populated agricultural district far beyond, made lovelier still by the soft gray veil of distance, handsomely diversified with highly cultivated vegetable, floral and horticultural gardens, and extensive and valuable plantations, intersected by numerous railways and graveled roads, present a most enrapturing prospect. Turning toward the "busy haunts of man," what a panorama of mingled art and nature meets the eye; church-spires are marshaled in hosts, and warehouses stud every quarter; the mansions of the opulent, half hid by ancestrial trees, and the cottages of the humbler citizens are seen in every direction; the smoke-stacks of industry rising at countless points, form a forest of progress, while the clouds of smoke vomited from their untiring throats bathe the city in vapory folds, and seem climbing one on top the other to kiss the "God of Day." Lastly, the river winding like a silver snake —not by bald and sky-kissing peaks, but past the scenes of honest toil and thrift, lending the force of its waters to turn the ponderous wheels of its shipping, and to add to the comfort of the people who inhabit its banks. There are no red gashes in the fair bosom of mother earth: swords in this quarter of the "moral vineyard," have been turned into plow-shares, spears into pruning-hooks—it remains only for the iron-tongued eloquence of the pen, more powerful than the gleam of falchion or the sceptre of kings—to proclaim its glittering excellencies and to assert its proud position. To witness these charmes and to feel the sublimity of the cause, there seems within the heart such a flood of melody seeking voice that some times, for very ecstacy, one is half tempted to give language to all the pent-up joy that other men have frittered away, and that we have garnered up for a sight so rare and exquisite. The poet, Cowper, had in his mind's eye a scene of comporting grandeur:

"'T is pleasant, through the loop-holes of Retreat,
To peep at such a world;
To feel the stir of the great Bable, and not feel the crowd;
To hear the roar she sends through all her gates
At a safe distance, where the dying sound
Falls a soft murmur on the uninjur'd ear."

So, whether we take it in the garish light of day, or under moonlight, or starlight vision, no city in the South presents a fairer view than Columbus, the Queen City of the South.

POPULATION.

In days immediately prior to the war, Columbus advanced with regularity, and, up to the commencement of hostilities it was a place of comparative importance. The greatest growth and increase in population, however, has been during those years intervening the close of the late struggle and the present time, and it has moved forward with bold impetus, not only in wealth and commercial and manufacturing magnitude, but in substantial and perceptible aggregation of resident population. In 1870, the first census taken after the war, Columbus contained a population of 7,401, and in 1880, 10,123. There was considerable disappointment, and we may say, chargin, among the boastful citizens, when the census of 1890 showed a population of only 18,650. In this connection we may say, too, that the census-taker is yet to see the light of earth who could give general satisfaction, and for this reason all census reports have been set down as notoriously imperfect. We, however, propose to be just a little charitable with the authorized enumerators, but to take sides with the people in this way: In the the first place, the Census Bureau, as at present conducted, is nothing short of a Government sinecure, glaringly faulty and speculative in the extreme. The enumeration is generally made during the summer months, at which time a large proportion of the urban population are "out of town." Their loss is never placed on the credit side of a community's numbers, nor do we find included in the reports many persons living in tenement houses, in back alleys, desultory dwellings, in basements or in attics. In view of these facts, we propose selecting three plans of calculation in determining the present population in the city, and while we depricate these comparisons which are proverbially "odious," we shall place sufficient confidence in the general correctness and utility of the figures to give them a place in this department of our report, asking for them a careful consideration as to plausibility:

PICNIC GROUNDS, NORTH HIGHLAND

First—According to the official vote of the city at an election where a full vote is cast, there were 3,500 votes polled. Estimating seven inhabitants to each vote, (instead of eight, as is generally customary), we have a total population of 24,500.

Secondly—There are eight thousand and nineteen names in the last City Directory for Columbus alone; estimating 3½ inhabitants for each name, and we find in this city a population of 28,067; add to this the population of Girard and Phenix City, 7,636, and we find that the city and suburban towns show 35,703 inhabitants.

Thirdly—Estimating 9,440 lots within the city limits (or eight lots to the acre), and three inhabitants to each lot (in Chicago and Philadelphia the rule which holds is six inhabitants to each lot, and ten lots to the acre), the city affords accommodation for 28,320.

There are a variety of means of accounting for this gratifying growth, and observant Columbusonians will readily believe it. The most prominent reason established is the fact that, our manufacturing interests having made such perceptible and gigantic strides of late, it has brought to us a greater addition of numerical strength than could have been the case had our trade been merely and only of a commercial nature. Nevertheless, we chose to accept even our own figures only with a grain of conservative salt, and to predict that the year 1900 will witness a *bona fide* population in the city of Columbus of 50,000 souls. Now, observe that we do not resort to the trick of percentage—a very untrustworthy method, since it is a less feat for a small town to grow twenty-five, fifty, or one thousand per cent. than for a great city to do the same—but having by three different rules of calculation, found an absolute addition to the city's population of an average of 8,310 souls which, added to the Federal census, gives us an average population of 26,960, may we not fairly and not ungreedily figure the increase the next eight years commensurate with that of the past two, calculating for the contribution of the country to the city, added to the city's own recruting power by birth—and the locality is certainly favorable to fecundity—legitimately entitling us to the better half of a *hundred thousand* at the close of the next decade.

THE MATRIMONIAL OUTLOOK.

Columbus, it would seem, is also a good place at which to "marry," provided, of course, the applicant is of suitable age, comes well recommended, is good-looking, sensible, industrious, and possesses a fair modicum of this world's goods and chattles; though these preliminary qualifications are generally settled by the parties most interested, and we have nothing to do with the business, only in a statistical form to present the city's advantages in this light. From April 1, 1891, to March 31, 1892, the total number of marriage license issued was 400. The number of divorce suits docketed for the May, 1892 term of Court was *six*, which proves conclusively that there are very few unhappy matrimonial alliances, and that a very large and gratifying percentage of those who copartnership their joys and sorrows, travel the rugged paths of life in full accord and sympathy.

CHARACTERISTICS OF THE PEOPLE.

The native Columbusonian is not the lean, lank, sad, intense, subjective Yankee, nor the dilatory, fatty, undemonstrative dullard of Pennsylvania; but he is always florid, plethoric, laborious, well-fed, jolly and complacent. He works like a dray-horse in daylight, and is a profound sleeper at night, open, loquacious, liberal, he patronizes "church festivals," and while yet a beau, congregates in scores at club dances. He is gallant to the ladies, attentive to strangers, and all in all, is a "duced clever fellow." He loves self-reliance as the son of Erin loved solitude, *ad est*, with his crony or his sweetheart. Whether he is a laborer or a banker, he manages to get away with three square meals per diem. He frequently wears a respectable mustache, generally shaves his chin, never wears gloves during business hours, always keeps the side-walk, owns his turn-out, which sometimes being a phaeton, he permits his matronly and excellent better-half to drive down and escort him homeward; he is an irreclaimable literary client of the *Enquirer-Sun* or *Ledger;* he takes great interest in politics, but never allows public matters to interfere with business; always goes to church on Sunday, and during the week patronizes amusements of first-class and acknowledged merit: in short, he is ever on the alert, and prone to do things that will promote the city's interest and glorify her commercial condition. Such a people are necessarily practical, since the executive faculty under such conditions is too important for work to allow attention to what is not visibly practical. It is attributable to such characteristics, perhaps, that our city has progressed and prospered as she has, for undoubtedly a fair degree of the very best enterprise of the country is seated in Columbus.

TRANSPORTATION FACILITIES.

The position of Columbus on the banks of the Chattahoochee river, gives her advantages which few cities of the South command. Her location with respect to the whole extent of the country embraced in the Chattahoochee Valley, and extending to that portion of the country traversed by the many streams tributary and made tributary to her by means of her river, is of such a peculiar character, that when viewed with reference to her natural means of intercourse with the States within these boundaries, she stands in a position both to demand and command the entire trade of this vast territory. The increasing demand for cheap transportation, and, in fact all transportation arising out of the multiplying wants of the growing population of the various sections of the nation, must, at an early day, cause the Chattahoochee to be made as fully available for transportation as it is possible for engineering skill to render it. The Chattahoochee is the dividing line between Georgia and Alabama, with a navigable length of 223½ miles: the Flint, with a length of 261 miles: and the Apalachicola, 137 miles, have shown each year a prompt return in the increase of commerce as the work of improvement went on; and what has been done in the past is but a slight indication of what will be the result when, with navigation unimpeded, and schedules of our boats as reliable as they will be, the country bordering on our streams settled with an industrious population, and all our country receiving the full benefit of these water-ways so favorably placed for use and benefit. The improvement of the navigation of the Chattahoochee has, in past years, been so strongly pressed upon Congress, that the Chattahoochee Valley Improvement Commission will no doubt soon perfect plans and secure an appropriation sufficiently large to enable them to make the river navigable at all seasons of the year.

RAILROAD INTERESTS.

To the railroad interests of the city, the past year has been of the utmost importance, as it has marked throughout the country a period of remarkable

HILTON—PROPERTY OF MUSCOGEE REAL ESTATE COMPANY, EAST HIGHLANDS.

prosperity to the railroads in general. During almost the entire year the roads concentrating in the city have been taxed to their full capacity, and in some instances beyond their facilities, to perform the work. Both passengers and freight have greatly increased, especially the former, and it may be stated, without any exaggeration, that the railroads in which Columbus is interested have never before been in a more prosperous condition. Not only has there been more to do, but the physical condition of the property has been better than at any previous period. The past few years have witnessed remarkable development, not only in the railroads actually running into Columbus, but in those that, in other Southern States, had apparently no definite termini, and formed merely a disjointed system of railways, each looking out for its own local interests. The great railroad manager of the age suddenly appeared in the field, and although he did not commence his work in this immediate section, his gigantic operations, whether in the North, West, the far West, or in Mexico, have all had a direct bearing upon Columbus The rapid manner in which he obtained control of road after road, and combined them into vast but harmonious co-operative systems, was suddenly followed in the South by several bold railway managers; and the product has been the combination of numerous short and weak roads into long and self-sustaining trunk lines, reaching from the lakes to the Gulf, from the Mississippi to the Atlantic. The establishment of these trunk lines has produced a wonderful activity in railroad circles, the benefits of which to the South in the purchase of new material, laying new and re-laying old tracks, securing a host of new locomotives and cars, and engaging thousands of additional employees, have been sustained by the competition natural between such strong and wealthy corporations to add new lines, new territory, and new trade to their resources.

THE GEORGIA CENTRAL RAILROAD.

The Georgia Central system stands more prominent than any other great system in the South, and it is largely due to the Central Railroad and Banking Company of Georgia that Columbus is to-day one of the most flourishing cities in the South. Instead of taking from Columbus her retail trade, the Central Railroad has enabled Columbus to become the great manufacturing centre that it is. It has given her prominence over other places to which she never could have attained with the miles of iron track, reaching out like so many arteries from the heart, over which course the pulses of trade as measured by the country. The Central system proper is 1,643 miles long, and embraces the following:

From Savannah to Macon	192	Montgomery and Eufaula	80
Macon to Atlanta	104	Mobile and Girard	85
Milledgeville to Gordon	17	Port Royal and Augusta	245
Columbus and Western	89	Upson County	16
Columbus and Rome	50	Savannah and North Alabama	60
Augusta and Savannah	53	Ocean steamship	250
Eatonton Branch	22		
Southwestern and Branches	321	Making Total	1,643

COLUMBUS AND WESTERN RAILROAD.

This road is a part of the Georgia Central system, and is one of the best equipped roads out of Columbus, and places this city in direct communication with Birmingham, Montgomery and Atlanta. At Birmingham it forms a connection with the Birmingham, Memphis and Atlantic Railway, thus making the shortest line from Kansas City to New York. By this road, Columbus is connected with all the important cities of the North-West on a direct line.

MOBILE AND GIRARD RAILROAD.

The Mobile and Girard Railroad is one of the most important tributaries to the city of Columbus. It is embraced in the Central System, and has been leased to the Central for a period of ninety-nine years. This road extends from Columbus to Troy, Ala., a distance of eighty-five miles, and in as good condition as any road in the country. The Mobile and Girard has been under the control of the Central for a number of years, and while this has been the case, the people of Columbus have much cause for congratulation in the liberal policy adopted. Since the road has been leased there is none other than the highest commendation for the course pursued, as it is believed that it will be for the best interest of the stockholders, the Central Railroad, Columbus and all concerned. There is a clause in the lease which gives the Central authority to extend it, if so desired, and as a commercial move it was to the interest of the Central to extend it, and it has been done.

GEORGIA MIDLAND AND GULF RAILROAD.

This road can be strictly called a Columbus enterprise, for it it is to the untiring efforts of some of her leading citizens that the road was built and equipped. The road was built by the Georgia Midland Construction Company, which was chartered by the State with an authorized capital of $1,000,000. The road extends from Columbus to Griffin, where it connects with the Georgia Central for Atlanta and all points in Southern Georgia, South Carolina and Florida. At Columbus it connects with the Alabama Western for Montgomery, Mobile, New Orleans and Texas: Columbus and Western for Birmingham, with the Mobile and Girard for Eastern and Central Alabama, and with the extension of this line to Albany will connect at that point with the Georgia Central for Savannah, with the Brunswick and Western to Brunswick, and with the Savannah, Florida and Western to Savannah, Fernandina and Jacksonville; at Jacksonville with the Florida Railway and Navigation Company to Cedar Keys, and the Jacksonville, Tampa Bay and Key West Railway to Tampa Bay, and thence by ocean steamer to Key West and the West Indies. It is the best built road to-day in the South, and has been constructed with such economy as to astonish even expert contractors. It has standard steel rails, iron bridges throughout, and is the smoothest roadbed and best equipped road in the South. It traverses the garden spot of Georgia, and a section of country that has only needed railroad facilities to develop the finest country in the South—a country of excellent water, exhilarating climate, productive lands and fine timber.

COLUMBUS AND ROME RAILROAD.

This is a narrow gauge, and extends from Columbus to Greenville, in Meriwether county. The road was originally contemplated to be built to Rome, a distance of 125 miles. The road is now operated to Greenville, and brings more cotton to Columbus annually than any of the other roads. It was asserted some time ago that this road would be extended to Atlanta, but if such a thing was ever contemplated it seems to have been abandoned. And this will, no doubt, be conceded a good thing for Columbus, as well as a wise one for the Central Railroad, as all the cotton in the sections of country contiguous to the line now finds its way to this market, and aids materially in swelling our receipts. The road is in splendid condition, and the amount of business done over it is enormous. It is an exceedingly popular road, is run under the right kind of management, and is a blessing to Columbus.

THE COLUMBUS SOUTHERN RAILWAY.

This road runs via Albany to Brunswick, and via Americus to Savannah. It is an important outlet for the city.

THE BUENA VISTA AND ELLAVILLE RAILWAY.

This is a part of the Georgia Central system, and extends to Americus. The road is now in complete running order, and has some important connections.

THE CHATTANOOGA, ROME AND COLUMBUS RAILWAY,

Is another important outlet to the city, and when fully completed to its intended terminus, will be of great value to the already large railway system of Columbus.

THE DUMMY LINE.

Connecting with all the railroads entering the city, is a Belt Dummy Line, owned by the Columbus Railway Company. It extends through the city and

MAGNOLIA—PROPERTY OF MUSCOGEE REAL ESTATE COMPANY, EAST HIGHLANDS.

suburbs, and is used for passenger trafic, and for delivering car-load lots of freight direct to and from the stores and mills of the city. The value of this line to the wholesale and manufacturing interests can scarcely be estimated, as it facilitates the handling of freights, and saves a large bill of expense for extra handling and hauling. The Company are so accommodating that they agree to put in side tracks in any portion of the city, into the yards or warehouses of any firm desiring them.

And now, with this wide-spreading, comprehensive system of transportation, together with our water facilities, to make tributary to our market the riches of the vast scope of country in which we are located, developing our own unrivaled resources, and distributing far and wide our products in manufactures and commerce, who can portray in word-picturing the grand and brilliant future in store for this beautiful city, or doubt that it is destined to rank prominent among the proud array of American cities whose towering strength makes them the marvel of the entire world.

COLUMBUS AS A COTTON MARKET.

This city has always ranked as the best cotton market in the South, and the receipts during the past year have demonstrated that she is holding on to her reputation. The cotton year closes on the last day of August, therefore, we can only give the official figures for 1890-91, taken from the *Enquirer-Sun* of September 1, 1891:

RECEIPTS.

Railroad	37.144
Wagon	29.148
River	22,560
Total receipts	88,852

COTTON SHIPMENTS.

By rail	66,333
By factories	19,041
River	2,774
Total shipments	88,148

STATEMENT.

Stock on hand August 31, 1889	500	
Received during 1889-90	88,152	—89,442
Shipments		88,148
Stock August 31, 1891		1,294

STOCK IN WAREHOUSES.

The following is the stock on hand at the various warehouses at the close of business last night:

Planters	205
Alston	61
Lowell	585
Fontaine	193
Webster	250
Total	1,294

THROUGH COTTON.

The through cotton since August 31, 1891, which is cotton shipped from other points, compressed in Columbus and shipped to Savannah, thence to New York, Eastern spinners and Liverpool, amounts to 96,502 bales, divided as follows:

Columbus and Western road	57,320
Mobile and Girard road	7,222
Columbus and Rome road	13,708
Western Railway of Alabama	17,947
Buena Vista and Ellaville road	305
Total	96,502

There are three compresses in this city, with a capacity of pressing 2,400 bales per day, and in the busy season they work both day and night.

There are seven large cotton warehouses in the city, with a capacity for storing 55,000 bales of cotton. These warehouses are substantially built, and made as near fire proof as it is possible.

THE JOBBING TRADE OF COLUMBUS.

In taking up this department of our labors, we propose demonstrating, so far as our power lies, the vantage ground Columbus occupies, and the facilities she possesses for the conduct of a successful commerce, not only respecting those articles of manufactured goods turned out from her industrial establishments. but to include all goods imported from other markets, whether of domestic or foreign production. Our mammoth establishments for the sale of dry goods, groceries, hardware, boots and shoes, drugs, queensware and all the articles that go to make up a general merchandise trade, contain immense stocks of every description, and are conducted by merchants of acknowledged probity, energy, intelligence and wealth— many of whom were engaged in business here previous to the war- while a host of new houses have sprung up, increasing competition and imparting renewed vigor to the sinews of trade, which were impaired by the terrible convulsions of civic strife. They have thus confidently entered the list of commercial rivalry with the merchants of the Eastern cities, having themselves perfected arrangements with the manufacturers of the United States and foreign countries, gaining facilities thereby of utmost importance.

Formerly, it was the custom of buying stocks twice a year (spring and summer, fall and winter), but this plan has been completely changed, and assortments are now kept up by making purchases oftener—say, every month or two—and the conclusion is, that "old goods" are rarely, if ever, on hand, and articles are not handled in the store six months, are kept cleaner and brighter and more attractive, If, then, the retailer who visits New York and the East cannot afford to go oftener than twice a year, he suffers loss by being "behind the fashion" if he does not go, and loses money and traveling expenses if he does go. If he is an experienced merchant he may perform the labor of selecting without any serious detriment; but even then it is a labor, and consumes all the difference in profit he would gain by purchasing in a nearer market. If he is inexperienced, he is likely to be led into the purchase of goods which will prove entirely unsalable, and the loss thereto incident may prove a serious drawback upon the success of a whole season's business. Hence, it is obvious that a purchaser of a miscellaneous stock, including everything adapted to the wants of a rural town or city population in the country, must be, when in Columbus, as near the most desirable market as it is possible for him to get.

The only practical question for a retailer to consider, then, is, whether it is probable he can make his purchases in the Columbus market as cheaply as in any other. This we assert he can do, and we leave it to the consideration of those who study and appreciate commercial economy. To our own personal knowledge it has been already forcibly and eloquently demonstrated. Is it not probable, then, that the merchants of Columbus, in view of their advantages, consignments from abroad seeking their shelves, with abundance of capital and good credit, can buy and sell on terms as favorable as any of their competitors?

There are a great many other local advantages that might be placed to the credit side of our account, but such as we have omitted here will be spoken of in detail in other portions of our book. Those we have considered, however, are entitled to the closest consideration of the country merchant.

THE WHOLESALE DRY GOODS AND NOTIONS TRADE.

The trade in dry goods, considered as a branch of commerce, is the most important of any now existing in this country. It controls a greater amount of capital, employs a larger number of persons, and contributes a greater value of commodities than any other branch of mercantile pursuit.

In the dry goods line, perhaps, more than any other, energy and capacity decide the success of the business man, for it is a business requiring great judgment in the selection of stock, as well as resolution in general management. To buy at the right time, and the right classes of goods to suit the trade, and in proper quantities, as well as to gather the custom to take the goods, require no ordinary class of ability. Commercial prosperity is largely due to the business men who control this interest, for they have shown a degree of ability and energy in building up the wholesale dry goods trade of this city surpassed nowhere in the country.

Our jobbing trade has a bright record for the past year: no failures, increase of territory yearly, a steady increase of sales, consequently increase of stocks and facilities of doing business. It to-day looks forward to the time when it will make Columbus the Southern market for dry goods and notions for the States of Alabama, Florida and Georgia. If push, capital, accommodation, stocks and prices to meet the wants of the trade mean anything, then it will be done in the near future.

Three exclusively wholesale and importing houses are engaged in the trade, besides thirty-three wholesale and retail, and retail houses, making a total of thirty-six houses engaged in the dry goods and notions business. The total business, according to the data we have obtained, foots up to the enormous sum of $3,787,943. Some of the retail establishments are mammoth concerns, several of them employing at least fifty clerks, etc., each. These stocks in general are of the finest and most fashionable kinds, and the stores are generally filled with customers.

THE WHOLESALE GROCERY TRADE.

In its wholesale branch, the grocery trade of Columbus engages the attention of more merchants than any other one vocation. In the city's crowded thoroughfares may be found its spacious warehouses, one day being filled, and the next day, as it were, emptied of their immense stocks, for, of all the mercantile pursuits, none surpasses this branch for vivasity and bustle. On every street and thoroughfare one encounters the throngs of well-laden drays and ponderous floats, rolling ceaselessly and noisily in their busy career, which, mingled and confused with the emphatic and sometimes profane ejaculations of the almost innumerable army of teamsters, and draymen, and porters, and laborers—all highly essential features of the trade—present a truthful panorama of a commercial Bable, yet everything moves with the regularity of clock-work.

LOVERS' LEAP, NORTH HIGHLAND PARK.

Splendidly arranged and capacious buildings, in keeping with the demands of the trade, have been erected in the leading marts New sections of country have been made tributary, until now the business stands out bold and prominent, symbolizing that eminent quality of go-aheadativeness that characterizes the Columbus wholesale grocery trade, either as individual firms, or taken as a fraternity. The total number of wholesale grocery firms in the city is thirteen, seven wholesale and retail grocers, making a total of twenty firms carrying on the wholesale grocery business. Besides these, there are one hundred and fifty-four retail grocers in the city, making a total of one hundred and seventy-four firms engaged in selling groceries in this city, the aggregate sales amounting to $6,284,312 per annum. Our wholesale grocery business is governed by capitalists and merchants of long experience, who supply themselves in largest quantities from original sources.

The low rates of freight to Columbus by car-load lots, strengthened by purchases of large invoices and their corresponding discounts, give our wholesale grocers the opportunity of dividing the goods to retailers and country merchants at as low or lower figures than small or moderate quantities can be bought at any other competing point. The rapidity with which goods can reach interior points obviates the necessity of laying in larger stocks than are wanted for immediate use, which is a very decided advantage to the retailer, as it prevents the accumulation of old stocks, which is a dead weight in business.

THE WHOLESALE CLOTHING TRADE.

Ready-made clothing in Columbus, as well as in all jobbing markets occupies an important position among business pursuits. It has extended to all sections of the country, limiting the country merchants' sale of piece goods for men's and boys' wear, compelling tailors, in some instances, to abandon their trade and embark in the business themselves, or seek other employment. The introduction of sewing machines to this class of work, has greatly facilitated rapid and durable manufacture, and brought clothing down in price to a wonderful degree. Country merchants, who have been careful in the selection of sizes and styles, have found that the sale of clothing can be effected with less trouble than piece goods, and without the serious drawback of remnants; that there is less competition; that their daily receipts of cash are thereby increased, as well as other advantages. Indeed, so satisfactory and lucrative has this business proven, that as an additional illustration of the tendency of the age to increased manufactured articles, mention may be made of shirt-making, and of those branches, including men's and boys' underwear, which form important adjuncts to the business. Connected with this department, gents' furnishing goods, embracing neckwear, handkerchiefs, gloves, hosiery, etc., etc., come in for a large share of attention.

The Columbus market will favorably compare in this respect with any in extensive and varied stocks, in quality, style, workmanship, "fit," reasonable price and fair dealing. Three firms in the city are wholesaling clothing, and there are quite a number of retail firms who are not averse to selling a bill to country merchants. The total business in clothing we estimate to be about $760,000 per annum.

WHOLESALE BOOTS AND SHOES.

Not less important than the wholesale clothing trade is that of boots and shoes, which has also had a wonderful growth in the last few years. Like the old, slow-coach method of making our wearing apparel by hand, the cobbler's bench, with its accompanying "kit," which, not many years ago, was an essential feature upon almost every plantation, as well as a fixture of every city, town or cross-road hamlet, has "had to go" the way of old-time customs. The advance of progress, with its powerful equipment of labor-saving machinery, hesitates not to destroy ruthlessly the well-loved images of our earlier recollections. But regrets are soon dissipated by the blessings which flow from what—at the time—is looked upon as tantamount to vandalism. This is fully demonstrated in the fact that ninety per cent. of the boots and shoes now worn are factory-made, and as a result the world receives compensation in a multitude of ways, and to an extent that could never possibly have been hoped for from the ancient system. The manifold benefits derived by our city from this important branch of business may be conceived, from the immense annual sales made by the dealers in this city, footing up over $1,250,000, and yearly being augmented by the expanding trade, which is reaching out in every direction through the country now tributary to us, and being added to by the further increase of transportation facilities There are thirty-nine firms selling boots and shoes in this city—two being jobbers. The stocks are all complete and suited to the wants of the Southern trade.

WHOLESALE HATS AND CAPS.

In this line we have one wholesale establishment, but the stock is carried in

RESIDENCE H. J. ABBOTT, EAST HIGHLANDS.

connection with dry goods and notions, but is full and complete, and sold at prices as favorable to the purchaser as any other Southern city can boast. Besides the house mentioned, we have nine firms engaged in retailing hats and caps in connection with other goods. The trade in this line is in an exceedingly prosperous condition, and the annual operations of the establishments engaged in it show that their growth is healthy, as well as rapid. The sales will average $500,000.

WHOLESALE DRUGS, PAINTS, ETC.

Long before the wholesaling of goods of this line was ever thought of as a distinct business, or even considered in combination with any other branch in this city, the great houses of the East had already established themselves firmly, as they thought, in the trade of this whole region of country; so that, for every dollar's worth of custom the houses of this city obtained, they had to contend with giants already in the field. The same condition of affairs, however, held good in all branches of our wholesale trade, but the enterprise, vim, and determined efforts of our drug men have resulted in the most pronounced success, just as the outcome of energies put in every other department has brought prosperity to those so engaged. Those houses dealing in this line have, by their skill as pharmacists and chemists, and their thorough knowledge of the wants of the people in the territory tributary to this city, succeeded in fully establishing themselves in the good estimation of their patrons, and building up a trade which will not in any wise suffer by comparison, relatively speaking, with the immense establishments of the large Eastern cities. Carrying nothing but the freshest and purest goods in the way of drugs, keeping every department in their line up to the highest standard, and with ample capital, their stocks are constantly enlarging, and their trade extending and growing heavier. There are two wholesale houses in this city, besides eighteen retail druggists. The annual transactions will average $682,000.

THE WHOLESALE LIQUOR TRADE.

The liquor business is one to be found every where, go where you will, and notwithstanding it is one which bears the unenviable reputation, in all quarters of the globe, as being a destroyer of mankind not without good reason, it is true and paradoxical although it may be, we find it not infrequently in advance of civilization, and *always* keeping abreast with the vanguard of progress. It is a source of undoubted wealth to all our cities, and contributes unquestioned strength and general prosperity to the commerce and industries of all communities. Candidly speaking, it is an evil, hydra-headed, and more venemous than the tooth of any serpent that drags its cold and clammy folds over the bosom of this kindly earth, when abused by fallen manhood, and it is this maltreatment of an article, which evidently was not created for a baneful purpose, and which we know contains elements highly beneficial to the world at large, that has brought odium upon the name, and woes unnumbered upon the human race, individually and collectively.

Fortunately, however, for our city, the trade has always been in the hands of perfectly honorable business men, and being not less enterprising and public-spirited than they are upright in character and dealings, they have succeeded in establishing an exceptionally high reputation for their business throughout the entire country tributary to the trade of this city. The stocks kept here equal those to be found in any city of the country in quality, both in imported and domestic goods, and they also compare favorably in extent, while the assortment is full and complete in all the various brands of wines, brandies and liquors. The high standard of goods has made this point a wholesale centre for the trade, quite extensive in proportions, and highly profitable to those engaged in it. The annual transactions foot up $480,000.

WHOLESALE HARDWARE, ETC.

This department of trade embraces hardware, heavy iron, steel, hollowware, tinware, etc., and very properly deserves a prominent place among the pioneer jobbing lines of the city, having been among the first to take the field against older and established points. However, it has advanced with steady strides, and is now one of the solid interests of the city. Experience has fully demonstrated the fact that it cannot only be carried on here with success in the face of all competition, but that it is one of the most prosperous and profitable lines of trade we have. Notwithstanding the formidable proportions the trade has already reached, there is abundance of room for a large increase of the business. Indeed, no point in the country offers better inducements than this as the centre of the hardware business. Last year the total sales amounted to not less than $630,000, and very possibly the actual total exceeds these figures. One thing is assured beyond all question of doubt, that the future of the trade here is of the most promising character, and must reach that high degree of prominence which the grand facilities of the locality will fully sustain, and which the entire country tributary to our market demands. There are five houses engaged in the wholesale and retail hardware business.

WHOLESALE CIGARS, TOBACCO, ETC.

There is a large business transacted in this city in the above lines. Nearly all of the wholesale grocers carry heavy lines of both foreign and domestic cigars, and all of the leading brands of chewing and smoking tobaccos. Then, there is one firm engaged exclusively in the wholesaling of tobacco and cigars. To separate this branch from the other lines dealt in would be an endless task, therefore, we can only approximate the sales and place them at $300,000 per annum.

MUSIC AND MUSICAL INSTRUMENTS.

Columbus has three houses engaged in the sale of music and musical instruments. Stocks are not only extensive, but represent the best quality of goods: rare collections of sheet music, adopted to all manner of instruments, with immense stocks of pianos, organs, melodeons, violins, flutes, guitars, banjos, accordeons, german silver, brass and field band instruments, strings, musical goods of every variety, from a reed fife to the most elaborately finished and finely cased rose-wood piano, representing all of the most popular and celebrated manufactures in the country, and brought to this city in all forms—grand, square and upright. The trade in this business will amount to fully $220,000.

BOOKS AND STATIONERY.

The character and standing of those houses engaged in this trade is well and favorably known throughout this section, and their enterprise and liberality to the trade has kept abreast of our great advancement. The business is in a healthy condition, and dealers report a large per cent. of gain over the business of preceding years.

THE FURNITURE TRADE.

There are a number of substantial firms engaged in the above business in

Columbus. The business is in the hands of men of probity and reliability. There are eight firms, whose annual transactions will reach $250,000.

FRUITS AND CONFECTIONERIES.

There is considerable business carried on in the above line in this city. The stocks carried are full and complete, and all kinds of fruit find a ready sale here. Our dealers are always in the lead in securing the first of the season, which commands good prices. In confections, the stocks carried are large and varied, and always fresh. The business is in the hands of honorable and upright dealers and will average $120,000.

MISCELLANEOUS.

In addition to the leading lines of the wholesale business which we have briefly alluded to, there are, of course, a large number of other branches, such as are always to be found clustered at a large wholesale centre, which contributes largely to the general prominence and financial prosperity of the community, and its commerce and industries.

But while we cheerfully accord to those varied lines of our commerce the meed of praise they so justly deserve for their generous contributions to the wealth of the city by their vast sales, annually aggregating millions of dollars, we have not the space to take them up separately and *seriatum*, giving to each the extended notice its intrinsic value so highly merits. Suffice it to say that they all are in an exceedingly prosperous condition, and that they are extending their trade in every direction with great enterprise and commendable energy.

In conclusion, it can be said with truth and pride that, as a wholesale point for the establishment of any branch of commerce, no city is this country can boast advantages superior to those centered in this particular portion of the Sunny South, and which are steadily building up—making broad, firm and solid the financial integrity, honor, wealth and enduring greatness of the Queen City of the South.

THE RETAIL TRADE OF COLUMBUS.

It is not expected that a detailed statement could be made of the retail trade here in its various departments. Such a paper, fully elaborated, would by far too greatly transcend the limits not already occupied in this work, delay its appearance, and demand a personal sacrifice of time and means which cannot now be entertained. Our patrons and readers will be content, we are certain, with a general outline of it, as furnishing an indication as to its extent and importance.

The benefits of a healthy and progressive retail trade to a city are not easily summed up or disposed of in a few words. It not only supplies the city and country demand, but the inducements which it offers bring hither thousands upon thousands of dollars from all portions of the surrounding country tributary to this market, by means of convenient railroads and river communication. Every species of goods, from the plain and common to the most superb and costly articles, are to be obtained here at prices which are the same as Eastern retail figures, and we believe every article in general use can be found. The retail merchants of this city are, as a body, men of intelligence and business qualifications, and constitute an element in our midst which adds much to the vigor, prosperity and growth of our city. Their establishments are scattered over every quarter— in the business centres and in the suburbs—everywhere a group of dwellings may be found, some enterprising retailer has set up his sign as a landmark of the extending frontiers of civilization, and while driving a good business for himself, is adding something to the grand aggregate of bustle and importance of the city. Although there are a great many of these houses keeping miscellaneous stocks, yet we feel confident the following figures will approximate the true number, and for the most part those that have not been mentioned before. Altogether there are about 33 firms retailing dry goods; boots and shoes, and leather, 37; clothing and furnishing goods, 10; drugs, 18; groceries, 158; saloons and restaurants, 38; bakers, 4; barbers, 21; blacksmiths, 11; butchers, 17; besides a numerous array of miscellaneous houses, so varied that it would be a herculean task to give a clear idea of their pursuits. After having made a careful summary, we are able to place the retail establishments, all

PIC-NIC PARTY AT LOVERS' LEAP, NORTH HIGHLAND PARK.

branches included, at not less than *six hundred and twenty-two.* We hardly feel like attempting an estimate of their business, for anything short of a complete census would be incomplete, for the man has yet to be born, and besides be vouchsafed prying qualities and inquisitiveness supernatural, to enable him to form any correct idea of trades where large dealers have a horror of tax-gatherers, and small dealers a penchant for making their business appear as large as possible, and oftentimes, swelling their volume beyond such reason that even a newspaper reporter would be put to blush: and yet, for the sake of a little mathematical calculation, even if we cut down the receipts of the houses to $50 per day each, for 300 days of the year, we have an annual miscellaneous retail trade of more than *nine millions of dollars.*

MANUFACTURES AND MANUFACTURING ADVANTAGES OF COLUMBUS.

CAUSES OF SUCCESS.

It is an axiom, as true as trite, that no city has been or can be permanently prosperous without manufactures. A prosperity based exclusively upon a commercial business must necessarily be ephemeral. A city which, for instance, depends upon any one or more of the great agricultural staples for support, business and growth is liable to become paralyzed in her energies and interests, not only by failure in the production of such staples, but from their diversion to other points where eligibility gives them the advantage and preference as markets. Such, also, are the fluctuations in the price of articles of produce that no certainty of successful operations can be relied upon, and when uncertain, feverish and exciting speculation underlies the business of any community or city, there is no guarantee of permanent prosperity: whereas, where manufacturing is carried on successfully there is a steady, healthful and substantial growth. These facts, then, however unwelcome they may be to strictly commercial men, prompt us to the consideration of Columbus as a manufacturing point.

The term *manufacture*, in its derivative sense, signifies *making by hand.* Its modern acceptation, is directly the reverse of its original meaning, and it is now applied more particularly to those products which are made extensively by machinery, without much aid from manual labor. The word, therefore, is an exceedingly flexible one, and, as political economist do not agree in opinion whether millers and bakers are properly manufacturers or not, we shall, if need be, take advantage of the uncertainty and consider as manufacturers what strictly may belong to other classifications of productive industry.

The end of every manufacturer is to increase the utility of objects by modifying their external form or changing their internal constitution, and that the labors of both millers and bakers effect these things stand undisputed. Political economists also divide the essential requisites of production into two parts, viz.: labor and appropriate natural objects. But when applied to manufacturing industry, "success," they say, "depends upon a variety, or rather combination of circumstances, partly moral and partly physical." Foremost among the former are freedom of industry and security of property. Happily for us that our republican form of government not only protects, but fosters and encourages industry, while true republican principles make its faithful pursuit the "open sesame" to the enjoyments of its manifold benefits: and property is adequately protected by governmental and legislative action, wherever honesty is the ruling policy. Another moral cause contributing, and in fact essential to eminence in manufacturing industry, is the general diffusion of intelligence among the people. By intelligence, in this connection, we do not mean merely the understanding necessary to enable an individual to become the maker or master of a machine

RESIDENCE OF GRIGSBY E. THOMAS, JR.

—for capacity to contrive and invent seems a part of the original constitution of man—but simply the exercise of his faculties in the application of practical improvements upon successful enterprise in invention or mechanical labor, and the approbation and rewards bestowed thereupon. The eminent position at present occupied by the New England and other manufacturing States, are due rather to their sound, intelligent and practical philosophy than to any physical advantages or original intellectual superiority.

As ingenious mechanics and rapid workmen the Anglo-Americans have no superiors. As skilled workmen in departments for which they have been specially educated, the English are celebrated. Regular and habitual energy in labor, however, is a characteristic of both. They have no life but in their work—no enjoyment but in the shop. What other races consider amusement, is no amusement to them. But in England and America there is a marked difference between the quality of the labor that can be obtained in the country and in the towns. In fact, in or near large cities only can labor of the first quality be obtained.

As iron sharpeneth iron, so a man sharpeneth the countenance of his friends; and away from the centres of population and competition the face looseth its sharpness and the hand its cunning. Cities are in nothing more remarkable than in their attractive, magnetic influence upon talent of every discription.

"The man who desires to employ his pen," observes Carey, "and who possesses only the ability to conduct a country newspaper, removes to the interior, while the man of talent leaves his country paper to take charge of one in the city. The dauber of portraits leaves the city to travel the country in search of employment, while the painter removes to New York or London."

Superior mechanics and dexterous workmen manifest a similar pre fer ence for cities and an abhorrence for isolation; hence, if for no other reason, extensive mechanical or manufacturing operations must be conducted at a great disadvantage in isolated localities.

Passing to the consideration of the *physical* causes of eminence in manufacturing industry, we remark: They are more obvious than the moral causes, but not more important. To produce manufactured goods of a given quality with the least expense being the great disidteratum, it follows that whatever contributes to economy in production, whaever saves labor, or transportation, or raw material, cannot safely be overlooked or dispised. But to investigate carefully all the circumstances that have an influence upon economical production would require a considerable volume and be foreign to our main inquiry. The physical advantages which have contributed to England's eminence in manufactures, and which, we think, would apply as well to our country, are epitomized by the *Edinburg Review* in the following summary:

"Possession of surplus of raw material used in manufacturing; the command of natural means and agents best fitted to produce power; the position of the country as respects others, and the nature of the soil and climate." "As respects the first of these circumstances," says the writer, "every one who reflects on the nature, value, and importance of our manufactures of wool, of the useful metals, such as iron, lead, tin, copper, and of leather, flax, and so forth, must at once admit that our success in them has been materially promoted by our having abundant supplies of the raw material. It is of less consequence whence the material of a manufacture, possessing great value in small bulk is derived, whether it be furnished from native sources or imported from abroad, though, even in that case, the advantage of possessing an internal supply, of which it is impossible to be deprived by the jealousy or hostility of foreigners, must not be overlooked. But no nation can make any considerable progress in the manufacture of bulky and heavy articles, the conveyance of which to a distance unavoidably occasions a large expense, unless she has supplies of the raw material within herself. Our superiority in manufactures depends more at this moment on our superior machines than anything else; and had we been obliged to import the iron, brass, and steel, of which they were principally made, it is exceedingly doubtful whether we should have succeeded in bringing them to anything like the present pitch of improvement."

"But of all the physical circumstances that have contributed to our wonderful progress in manufacturing industry, none has had nearly so much influence as our possession of the most valuable coal mines. These have conferred advantages upon us not enjoyed in an equal degree by any other people. Even though we had possessed the most abundant supply of the ores of iron and other useful metals, they would have been of little or no use, but for our own almost inexhaustible coal mines."

NORTH HIGHLAND PARK DRIVE.

Water power was for a long time considered cheaper, especially for small manufacturing establishments, than steam power, but eminent engineers have carefully investigated the subject, and are of the opinion that in any position where coal can be had at "ten cents per bushel," steam is as cheap as water power at its minimum cost. Steam, therefore, until superceded by some more effective agent, will be the power principally relied upon to propel machinery, and as wood for the generation of steam upon an extensive scale is out of the question, we may safely conclude that at no very distant day the centre of our manufactures will certainly be in or near a district possessing inexhaustible supplies of cheap coal.

While we concede that coal is a more useful agent in manufactures, still it is equally as essential that the supplies of raw material be near at hand, and we assert that it is cheaper to transport the coal to Columbus, even from Tennessee, and there is plenty of it nearer, than to send the raw cotton to New England to be made up. And so it is, despite the pre-eminence of New England, her glory is destined soon to be overshadowed, for the sceptre will, ere long, depart from Judah and fall into the hands of the cities of the South, for the virtues which make a great people are indegenious to our soil, and will animate and ennoble our population whenever our capitalists and ingenious men have given its great physical advantages the fulfillment of this "manifest destiny."

With regard to the third point, viz.: favorable situation as respects commerce with other countries, its importance is second only to that which we have just considered. It is in the nature of manufactures to be regardful of its markets, and to supply with cash the demands of these, as well as to obtain the raw material on easy terms. Therefore, it is highly important that there should be a complete communication with all parts of the adjacent country by rail or river, and establish commerce, or facilities of commerce therewith.

A suitable climate is also a consideration of very great importance. The influence of climate upon the productiveness of industry, especially in manufactures, is very marked. In very cold climates the powers of nature are benumbed, and the difficulty of preserving life overrides all consideration for making existence comfortable. Climate has also a direct influence upon the durability of buildings, the workings of machinery, etc., and thus becomes an element of important consideration in many kinds of manufactures. Most writers on the subject insist that the soil of a country or district well adopted to manufactures need *not* be naturally very fertile, for when the soil is naturally so rich that agriculture is an easy art, it will not afford sustenance to many kinds of manufactures. This, to us, seems a mistaken idea, for it is reasonable to suppose that the cost of transportation to and from manufactories, outside, and we might say, far removed from the districts abounding in raw materials that enter largely into manufactures, could be obviated by the erection of similar manufactories nearer to hand.

Let us now pass to examine the claims of Columbus to the position of a manufacturing centre. While we do not claim that this city has all the requisites for a general manufacturing city, we do claim that for certain articles of manufactured goods we possess all the advantages necessary for the successful prosecution of such business. The centers of wealth, population and intelligence in the South are not numerous. Communities abounding in iron are few, but we have the raw material, the cotton, the wool, the timber.

Our numerous streams roaring seaward as they go by fields white with the snow of Southern summers, have been long calling to us in vain to allow them to join in the universal anthem of social industry. Capitalists of Columbus saw the advantages for large cotton factories, and they have been built, a description of which will be found on another page of this work. The profits of well conducted Southern factories are so certain and so great that the conversion by us of every pound of cotton into fabric is a mere question of time. The supply is, or could be, almost infinite; and that the demand for cotton fabrics in the same ratio, grown within sight, as it were, of the factory walls, would cost the manufacturer much less than it does his Eastern rival, even at its minimum value at the mills of the latter. The wool of Georgia is unsurpassed; flax, hemp and tobacco yield the best of crops. Nearly all of the cereals of the United States grow in Georgia. Almost all of the valuable varieties of forest trees grow in abundance in close proximity, and are of easy access by rail or river. In fact, the view is propitious for the manufacturer and for the establishment of manufactures from every standpoint. The motives of freedom, the fertility of soil, salubrity of climate, facilities for commerce and manufactures, and ease of railroad and water transportation, are the natural advantages which invite the capitalist, the tradesman and the manufacturer of every clime and nationality to a

FRENCH PLACE—PROPERTY OF MUSCOGEE REAL ESTATE COMPANY, EAST HIGHLANDS.

home in our midst, to co-operate in the development of its measureless resources, and to an inriching participation in its prosperity.

IMMENSE WATER POWER.

Before quitting the subject of manufactures, it is proper to say that Columbus has a water power that is a wonder of the land—that of the Chattahoochee river, extending northward over forty miles. It is equal to 1,000,000 horse power for the lowest stage, and nearly double that for the average stage. Only a small portion of this vast power is now utilized. Only one-tenth of the available power near the city is now in use, and the field is a most inviting one for the establishment of all kinds of manufacturing industries. In this connection, it is a pleasure to state that free sites with railroad frontage will be donated all worthy manufacturing institutions that desire to locate here.

COTTON AND WOOLEN GOODS MANUFACTURERS.

Columbus has long been the largest cotton manufacturing city in the South, having gained for herself the sobriquet of the "Lowell of the South," but we we prefer to call her the "Queen City," for she will lead in other manufacturers.

Columbus in the manufacture of Cotton goods is rather peculiar in that all its mills manufacture finer grades of goods than those usually made in the Southern factories, embracing cotton blankets, terry cloths, the celebrated Mitcheline quilts, sewing threads, cordage of many varieties, ginghams, cottonades and tickings. Three years ago the Paragon Mills were built, and as an experiment, embarked in the manufacture of the finer grades of ginghams, plaids, etc. The success of the venture has been clearly demonstrated and the Paragon has taken its place among the most successful cotton mills in Columbus. It cannot be denied that the cotton mills must eventually come to the cotton fields, and the history of mills in Columbus is but another link in the chain of evidence which so clearly establishes this fact.

The tabulated statement which appears below will give some interesting information in reference to the cotton mills of the city.

Names of Mills	Looms	Spindles	Hands Employ'd	Cotton Used Daily	Capital and Surplus
Eagle and Phenix Manufacturing Co...	1.800	60.000	2,000	50 Bales	$ 2.225.000
Muscogee Manufacturing Co...........	426	9,000	500	9 "	300.000
Swift Manufacturing Co...	360	8,000	400	9 "	200,000
Paragon Manufacturing Co............	300	....	300	5 "	100.000
Clegg Manufacturing Co	100	....	100	2½ "	50.000
Brown's Cotton Factory.......	....	4,000	80	4 "	80.000
†Chattahoochee Knitting Mills.........	*200	....	300	....	50,000
Totals	3.486	81.000	3.680	79½ B'ls	$ 3.100.000

†Owned by Eagle and Phenix Mills. *Machines.

REAL ESTATE HOLDINGS.

The list below gives the real estate holdings of the cotton mills of Columbus. Machinery and stocks are exempt from taxation and are not included in the figures named below:

Eagle and Phenix Manufacturing Company, mills and tenements..............	$ 729.000
Muscogee Manufacturing Company	147,000
Swift Manufacturing Company..	72,000
Paragon Manufacturing Company......................................	40.000
Clegg Manufacturing Company..	20,000
Browne's Cotton Factory..	15.000
Chattahoochee Knitting Mills.......................................	30,000
Total....	$1,053,000

The above figures by no means represent the total wealth of the cotton mills of the city. They simply give the value of real estate held by the several companies, as taken from the books of the city assessors for the year 1891.

Thus, it will be seen that Columbus has some large establishments manufacturing cotton and woolen goods, giving employment to 3,680 hands, to whom is paid annually the large sum of $1,766,400.

BARREL MANUFACTURERS.

There is one large establishment engaged in the manufacture of barrels, kegs, etc., in this city. The quality of the work turned out is equal to that of any city in the South, and the entire output finds a ready sale in the local and near markets to Columbus. The company employs a large force of men, and pay out annually as wages $18,200, while the annual sales will amount to $100,000. A more extended notice will be found on page 85 of this work.

BOOK BINDERS AND BLANK BOOK MANUFACTURERS.

There is one large establishment engaged in the manufacture of blank books. They have in connection with the same concern, a mammoth job printing office, paper box manufactory, etc. Employment is given to a large force of both male and female employes. The annual business will approximate about $50,000.

BREWERIES.

The reputation of Columbus beer has continued to strengthen ever since the plant was started, and at the present time the malt liquors made in Columbus, known as the "Chattahoochee Beer," takes precedence in every market where it has been introduced. We have taken pains to give an extended notice of this enterprise in another portion of our book, and we call particular attention to it. The business runs up into the thousands each year.

BRICK MANUFACTURERS.

There are four concerns engaged in the manufacture of building brick, tile, etc., in this city. Some of the establishments are mammoth concerns, and turn out as many as 100,000 brick per day. The business is in a healthy, growing condition, and, will no doubt, be largely increased during the coming year, as the outlook for a large number of new buildings is promising. The annual business will amount to $120,000.

CANDY MANUFACTURERS.

Columbus has two establishments engaged in the manufacture of candies, etc. Besides these there are a number of small concerns that make the cheaper grades of candy, such as taffy and common stick. On account of these small concerns we are unable to give reliable figures as to the transactions. As near as we are able to we place the total business at $50,000 per year.

CARRIAGE AND WAGON MANUFACTURERS.

The manufacture of carriages and wagons is extensively carried on in this city, there being no less than three firms engaged exclusively in their manufacture. Some of them are quite large, and the work turned out is first-class. The annual sales will reach about $45,000.

CIDER AND VINEGAR.

There is one large concern in this city manufacturing cider and vinegar, a more extended notice of which will be found in another portion of this work. The quality of the goods made has a wide-spread reputation for its purity, no

RESIDENCE OF MR. T. F. SMITH, NORTH HIGHLAND.

adulteration of any kind being permitted in its manufacture. The business is in a flourishing condition and steadily growing.

CIGAR MANUFACTURERS.

Columbus has three establishments engaged in the manufacture of cigars, and the product manufactured here is conceded to be equal to any manufactured in the State. True there are many larger manufactories in the State than will be found in this city, but in none of them is a better quality of cigars made than right here. The business will reach about $35,000 yearly.

CLOTHING MANUFACTURERS.

One great benefit to the community resulting from the manufacture of clothing is the immense field of employment it opens up for the poor, especially for females. There are a large number of firms manufacturing clothing in this city, and three of these deserve special mention, as their operations are carried on on a large scale, making goods for wholesaling. The prices paid employees, it is true, are not a very munificent remuneration for labor, but by respectable clothiers no advantage is taken of the necessities of the helpless. Exceptional cases there undoubtedly are, in which the poor are oppressed, but we are convinced the business principles of our respectable clothiers accord with the principles of humanity, and that the females they employ are paid reasonably fair prices. The annual sales will reach $225,000.

FERTILIZERS.

There is one firm in this city engaged in the manufacture of fertilizers, the annual sales of which are $100,000. Besides this there are several firms dealing in fertilizers manufactured at other points, which will run the total transactions up to over $275,000 per annum.

FLOUR AND GRIST MILLS.

In enumerating the various manufacturing industries of this city, we come to that of flour and meal. By disregarding the conflicting opinions of political economists as to their legitimate right to such classification, we present our readers with the statistics of one of the most important industries in Columbus. It is not many years since the idea of establishing a flouring mill in Columbus was hooted at as an absurd innovation. Exchanges in rival cities ridiculed the temerity of the venturesome miller who would dare erect his smoke-stack so far away from the grain supply, but the attempt was made, and the venture to-day is far beyond the experimental stage. We have two mammouth mills here, which do an annual business of many thousands of dollars, gives employment to a number of persons, many of them skilled workmen. The machinery is the latest and most improved that can be found, and the product equal to any in the United States.

IRON MANUFACTURES.

The advantages to be found at this point by the iron industries, although not yet developed to anything like the magnitude that circumstances and surroundings will justify, have still been utilized to a very considerable extent by far-seeing, enterprising men, who, by their energy, genius and go-ahead, determined spirits have established their business on a firm, paying basis, and which is constantly being expanded, bringing in return for the generous outlay of capital, wisdom and pluck, the golden prosperity their sturdy industry so richly merits. One of these establishments in particular will compare most favorably, indeed, with any works of the kind in the country, having ample facilities of the most improved order for turning out any description of mill and engine work, and, in fact, all grades of both light and heavy manufactures. Possessed of an abundant capital to increase their capacity to any extent made necessary by the demands of their rapidly growing trade, the annual augmentation of business is plainly evident in the constant increase to their already vast army of employees, and also in the wide distribution of the product of this skilled labor. But what is true of this one concern applies with equal force to all the establishments engaged here in *any* branch of the iron industry. The prosperity is abundantly demonstrated by their unceasing operation, the large force of operatives constantly employed, the steady growth of capacities for production, and solid financial condition of every firm connected with the trade. The vast extent of territory tributary to this point, and the rapid broadening of the scope which must make our city a base of

RESIDENCE OF TOL. Y. CRAWFORD, EAST HIGHLANDS.

supplies, together with the excellent character of all other necessary facilities and special advantages required by every department in the iron business to be found here, makes Columbus an unusually favorable locality in which to invest capital for prosecuting this highly important industry.

ICE MANUFACTURERS.

There are three companies in this city engaged in the manufacture of ice, which finds a ready sale in the local markets, besides large shipments are made to interior towns. The quality of the ice made in our factories is of the best, the water here being considered the purest that can be found in the State. The business will average about $75,000.

BAGGING MANUFACTORY.

Columbus has the only bagging mill in the State of Georgia, and it is the largest institution of the kind in the South. The factory has a capital stock of $75,000, and daily converts 6,000 pounds of jute into 3,000 yards of bagging, which finds ready sale throughout the cotton belt. The factory employs 100 hands, most of whom are females. The annual transactions will foot up $275,-000.

DRUGS AND CHEMICALS.

The manufacture of chemicals in Columbus is carried on quite extensively, almost every druggist in the country manufactures some special preparations for the benefit of his local custom, but the celebrity of these preparations scarcely, if ever, attains unusual runs. A striking exception to this fact are the medicines made by the W. W. C. Company and others in Columbus that we might name. There are four firms engaged in the manufacture of medicines whose annual transactions will foot up $100,000.

GRANITE AND MARBLE WORKS.

This industry is in a thriving condition in this city. The rare skill of the artizans engaged, together with superior quality of the marble and granite used, which comes, principally from Tennessee, North Carolina and the imported from Italy, has given Columbus a name throughout the whole extent of country tributary to her, and sales are made at all of these points. The annual transactions will average $60,000.

SASH, BLINDS AND DOORS.

The large amount of building in the city makes thriving times for the manufacturers of sash, blinds, and doors, moulding and stair work. There are five factories in the city, employing a large number of hands. The product is not consumed entirely by Columbus. The trade extends into the States of Georgia, Florida and Alabama. There is a constant growing demand for these manufactures that is very encouraging to new capital to locate here.

PLUMBING AND GAS FITTING.

This branch of Columbus' industries is prosecuted with great zeal and enterprise, the field being large and the demand rapidly increasing under the stimulating effects of general prosperity at home, and the constant development of the South. Tinware, though made a specialty by several manufacturers is also turned out in the large plumbing establishments. Five concerns occupy this field of industry, contributing over $100,000 to the grand aggregate of our manufactures.

But limited space forbids our going further into the details of the industries of this enterprising, go-ahead city, or the magnificent advantages each enjoy, however entertaining the task would be. Suffice it to say that under a heading of

MISCELLANEOUS.

can be grouped every discription of industry, (not specifically mentioned in the foregoing pages), that can be prosecuted at any point in the country, with the assurance that they will be found existing in Columbus in some stage of development. Many are worthy of extensive mention, for they are indispensible factors in the make-up of a great city, and have aided not a little in establishing the fame of Columbus, as may be inferred from brief allusions to such lines as trunk and valise factories, bakeries, sausage making, gunsmiths, blacksmiths, mineral and soda water factories, etc. These innumerable miscellaneous pursuits support vast numbers of our population, and though many of them may be conducted on a very modest scale, in some very retired spot, not one of them is to be sneered at, for all are noble, and help to swell the aggregate of our material wealth, thereby conferring special benefits upon the masses, the intrinsic value of which is inestimable.

GENERAL SUMMARY.

In reviewing the business interests of Columbus, we have borne in mind that our task was to give them a fair and impartial showing, and to benefit the community at large by stating *facts* that could readily be verified to the entire satisfaction of the world. Having set forth in their proper order these stern truths concerning the wonderful progress and substantial worth as a centre of commerce, trade and manufactures, it now remains to demonstrate their vast influence by combining their powers and presenting them to the view as a grand whole—a grand review, as it were, of the whole phalanx that has placed the crown of victory upon Columbus, and elevated it to its present high position amidst the surroundings of peace and prosperity. The annual transactions are shown in the following tabulated statement:

Wholesale and Jobbing Trade	$ 16,529,255
Manufactures	11,885,000
Retail Trade	9,000,000
Grand aggregate	$37,414,255

This magnificient showing is the result of industry, perseverance, economy, skill and progressive energy in a community of people, who, less than a quarter of a century ago were pennyless and powerless, with its city prostrate in the ashes created by the better hatred of civil war that hesitated not to sacrifice friend and foe alike in the agony of its expiring thores. What city in the annuals of history ever achieved grander results in so short space of time. When the great metropolis of the West was laid in waste by the fire fiend, and its people left homeless and starving, its annihilation was thought complete, and its restoration impossible. But while its inhabitants were still fleeing before the wrath of the destroying enemy, the world outstretched its loving hand to succor and to save. Even the remotest hamlet was eager in the good work, and the most uncompromising foe was touched with pity that put to flight all thoughts but those which prompted relief for the helpless. The result of such an outpouring of sympathy —demonstrative of the power of "Peace on earth and good will to man"—was quickly manifested in the sudden rise of Chicago to a state of grandeur, that makes it more truly than ever the phenominal city of modern ages and the astonishment of all who visit it. Compare Columbus with Chicago. Analyze every feature of their respective conditions at the date of the down fall of each, and every step in their progress to restoration—Chicago with the *entire world* for a friend, Columbus left to drink the last dregs in the cup of bitterness, and struggle onward alone—and then, if you can, deny that the metropolis on the banks of the Chattahoochee has won a nobler victory and a prouder record than the metropolis on Lake Michigan's front.

BANKS AND OTHER FINANCIAL INSTITUTIONS.

Columbus has four National and three State Banks, making a total of seven, with a capital of $650,000, and deposits amounting to upward of three and a half millions of dollars, and a surplus and undivided profits of nearly $300,000.

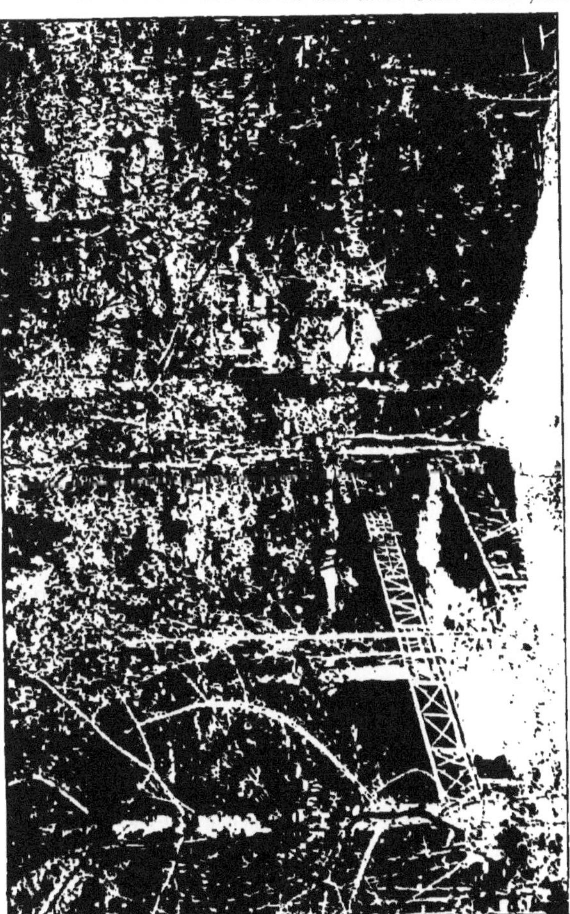

RUSTIC BRIDGE, NORTH HIGHLAND PARK.

OTHER INSTITUTIONS.

There are in Columbus a number of important Land and Investment Companies and Building and Loan Associations, which are proving valuable factors in the up-building of the city, and are receiving liberal support and encouragement from her people. The names of some of the leading Companies, together with their actual and authorized capital, are given below:

Company	Capital
Interstate Building and Loan Association	$7,500,000
Georgia Home Insurance Co. (total assets)	1,000,000
Muscogee Real Estate Co. (authorized capital)	1,000,000
North Highland Company	150,000
Columbus Investment Company	500,000
Muscogee Mutual and Columbus Mutual Loan	420,000
City Land Company	100,000
Rose Hill Company	75,000
Total	$10,745,000

THE COLUMBUS BOARD OF TRADE.

The following address, delivered by Mr. L. H. Chappell on assuming the duties of President in January, 1892, gives a brief history of the Columbus Board of Trade, which is composed of the leading business and professional men of Columbus:

It is idle, gentlemen of the Columbus Board of Trade, for one entering upon the office of President of this Board to attempt to express, in well-rounded sentiments, his appreciation of the honor conferred. His acts, and not his words, must tell the story of his fitness, and his devotion to the true interest of Columbus must indicate the sense of obligation and duty with which he accepts the trust—a trust which none among us would accept did we not feel that the obligation to heartily co-operate for the accomplishment of our common purpose is mutual, and rests alike upon each member of this Board, and upon every loyal advocate of the interests of Columbus. With this co-operation success is assured; without it, failure must be the portion of the ablest among us. The Columbus Board of Trade is habituated to success, and success has uniformly marked the career of those who have, in the ten years of its existence, administered its affairs, while their individual triumphs in Columbus was in the phenomenal development of our natural advantages. The first President, ten years ago, was G. Gunby Jordan, a man whose very name has become a synonym of strength and progress and success, and from whose massive brain and indomitable energy we have seen spring into existence a half score of corporations, employing an aggregation of millions of capital, and carrying the fame of Columbus into every State in the Union, and into the financial centers of the world. Next came J. W. Woolfolk, now the leading promoter of important enterprises in the capital city of our neighboring State. Next, the beloved and lamented Hochstrasser, a gentleman who stamped the impress of his exalted character upon every act of his life. Next, J. K. Orr, whose counsel is ever sought in the affairs of our city, and who never fails to respond with heart and hand, encouraging the timid and aiding the strong and brave. Next, Mr. C. E. Caverly, who comes to us flushed with success achieved in the wonderful Gate City of the South, and who blends so harmoniously the genius of his former with the genius of his present home. Finally, our retiring President, to whom this board owes, perhaps, a deeper debt of gratitude than to any of his predecessors, since to him we are indebted for our existence as a corporation, backed by a capital which insures our perpetuation independently of the limit of human life. At no time in our municipal history has there been greater need for the concert of action than at present. The beginning of the year 1892 finds the South struggling to recover from the effects of financial disturbances. They may be owing to the revolutions in South America and the consequent failure of the Baring Bros. in London, impairing confidence and credit throughout the financial world: or they may be the consequences of extravagance and over-trading during the flush times of '89 and '90: or it may be the over-production and low price of cotton: or it may be the McKinley Bill. Whatever the cause, there is no question about the fact that the times are hard. North and South have felt it alike, and no city has been exempt. Columbus, in the midst of it all, has continued to progress. It may not be christian-like, but there is a great consolation in being able to look around at our neighboring cities and say thank the Lord, we are not as bad as they. Instead of bank failures, we have a new bank opening, and another doubling its capital. Instead of railroad receivers we have a new suburban line opened—one of our new railroads reaching out for the snows of the North, and another for the orange blossoms of

RESIDENCES POLK HARRIS AND JOHN H. HENDERSON, EAST HIGHLANDS.

Florida. These evidences of progress and prosperity in times of stagnation and depression are the legitimate results of conservatism and co-operation and mutual confidence.

So long as we adhere to these principles we have nothing to fear. The same causes which have guided us away from disaster in times of depression will lead us on to the achievment of grand results in the flush times of prosperity, which will as surely follow as the flood tide follows the ebb.

REAL ESTATE INTERESTS IN COLUMBUS.

The condition of the real estate market during the past few years has been one of steady increase in values. All classes of real property have advanced in value, and the prices of to-day, as compared with those of past years, show an average advance of from 25 to 50 per cent. The heaviest demand for property, however, has not been from the capitalists and speculators, but from persons desiring homes or places of business for their own occupancy. Never, perhaps, in the history of our city have our people been so thoroughly possessed with the determination to own their own homes. This idea seems to have become incorporated in the warp and woof of every man's life, and to be the object of his exertions in business. This is not confined to one class of our citizens, but comprehends and permeates all classes and conditions. The demand covers every class of property, from the most palatial residence and handsomest stores in our city to the humblest and cheapest house known to the business. Our merchants and professional men who have long since owned comfortable, staid residences, and whose prosperity now warrants something different, are now purchasing more modern sites or buildings further North or East, and by building and remodeling, securing for themselves residences more in keeping with their increased means and advanced idea of comfort and elegance of the present day. The man of more moderate means, who has heretofore rented, is straining every nerve to own his own home and rent no more.

Real estate has been too much neglected by *investors*, and in the mad rush for wild-cat speculative stocks and bonds, the staid old investment has been left for a soberer period when the excitement of speculation had spent itself. That time is now upon us, and the panic which some of our wiseacres see dimly (?) in the distance is but the bursting of some of the bubbles of their own inflation, and cannot from the very nature of its everescent character, be widespread or general in its effects. Even over *guaranteed* stocks and bonds—all of which are now at a high rate of premium—does real estate possess positive advantages. The permanent character of it is an investment, the appreciation in value which it must experience in a growing country, the better rate of net interest it pays, all recommend real property over personal. The fact that it is not subject to such violent and frequent fluctuations, and is beyond the control of directors and syndicates having power to reduce its value to a minimum price without let or hindrance, is a powerful factor for inducing men to leave the uncertain ways of incorporated stocks in favor of this class of property.

Another reason for the advance in the price of property in this locality is found in the advance in rents during the past few years. This advance was a healthy one, predicated upon the law of supply and demand, and made necessary by the reduction which had taken place after the war, as a result of that calamity. We are all forced to study economy in some measure, and the item of house rent is the first to receive attention at the hands of most men. The conclusion is then easily reached that it is an economic measure to save the *profits* realized by the owner of the house. The desire follows to be your own landlord, and the realization is made possible through the poor man's helper, the loan association. These institutions have been of incalculable benefit to Columbus. The results of their work is the building up of nearly all that part of the city known as Rose Hill and East Highlands. Many a man in our midst owns his own home, who, but for their assistance, would now be a hewer of wood and a drawer of water, paying out the larger part of his monthly earnings for a shelter for his family, and barely eaking out an existence.

These associations have been of great help to men of larger means, who could afford to pay a considerable out per month in order to secure a comfortable home, but who could not afford to jeopardize their business by taking out the amount necessary to build a home from their own capital. Again have these associations been useful in assisting men to accumulate wealth in the matter of purchasing or building that class of houses which very nearly or entirely pay their own way through the loan associations, and at its termination leave them possessed of the property clear. In this way have some of our citizens amassed wealth, and added materially to the taxable property of the city. In these ways,

HICKORY HILL PROPERTY MUSCOGEE REAL ESTATE COMPANY, EAST HIGHLANDS.

and in others, have loan associations become important factors in building up our city, and increasing the demand for real estate by simplifying and attaining of it. In the consideration of the subject of real estate in Columbus, sufficient prominence has not been given to our improved condition as a community, as one of the elements of strength in the market. The financial solidity for which Columbus has always been noted is greater and more stable to-day than it ever was. While we have fewer millionaires than some communities further North, yet we are in a better condition, because the wealth of the city is more evenly distributed, and there are a great number of persons possessing moderate means and fewer extremely wealthy. The increase of wealth by slow accumulations gives as a population with a vast purchasing ability. The tax digest unfortunately is not the means of acquiring this information. But daily operations on the street will prove it, as will the presentation of any scheme which promises safe returns and good management call for the ample and liberal responses of capital. Columbus is rich in her resources of capital, and the best informed upon the subject know that the custodians of it are not to be found only in the recognized marts of the city, but frequently in unpretentious corners.

THE ENVIRONS OF COLUMBUS.

We have before remarked the thickly populated condition of the suburbs, in each direction, each quarter possessing some elements of beauty and attractiveness. Property, consequent upon the large influx of population that Columbus has received in the past few years, has so increased in value that space has become a costly luxury, only to be enjoyed by the more extravagant. In fact many persons who constitute a moving power, and a large proportion of our commercial and manufacturing world, are compelled to seek homes in some one of the many suburban towns that cluster around the metropolis and are vitalized by its proximity. They are as follows:

EAST HIGHLANDS.

THE PROPERTY OF THE MUSCOGEE REAL ESTATE COMPANY—THE MOST DESIRABLE RESIDENCE PROPERTY IN THE SOUTH.

There are two points which particularly impress every stranger who visits Columbus—the extreme desirability of its eastern slope for delightful and pleasant homes, and the astonishingly reasonable prices at which such property can be bought. Nor do they fail to note its many facilities for cheap and pleasant living, coupled with the fact that every dollar of this property must double, and probably treble, in value, while its owner occupant has the use of it as a home. Occupying (by actual measurement) the highest ground on the Georgia side of the beautiful and fast flowing Chattahoochee river, it is the most delightful place for a home that can be found. Here in ante-bellum days the merchant prince and wealthy planters made their homes, surrounded by all the luxuries that fancy could dictate and money purchase. A number of these old Southern homes still adorn the East Highlands. The Muscogee Real Estate Company was organized October 23d, 1887, by John F. Flournoy, Louis F. Garrard, and others of Columbus, with prominent capitalists of Savannah, Ga., Richmond, Va., and Rochester, N. Y. This company is different from most of the land companies organized in the so-called boom towns. Its lands were all paid for cash. Its stock is fully paid up, and none of it has been offered on the market. No auction sale of lots has been necessary, but a steady, solid, substantial growth has been encouraged. Since the material for the first new house was placed on the ground, October 27, 1888, there has been no time that a dozen new and handsome houses have not been under construction. There has been no wild speculation. The lot purchasers have been, as a rule, "home builders," and the hundreds of new and attractive homes which dot "*The Highlands*" attest the wisdom of the policy.

During the summer of 1888, the company commenced the development of their property by clearing the lands, opening the streets, etc. How well they have succeeded is told in a brief paragraph taken from the *Enquirer-Sun* of August 31, 1890: "The development of the East Highlands within the past year is simply wonderful. The originators of the enterprise gave the signal for the breaking of the old routine improvement plan, and opened a world of progres-

RESIDENCES OF C. E. DRUMBOR AND F. R. YOUNG—EAST HIGHLANDS.

sion and rapid growth, and kindled that fire of enthusiasm which has marked every successful enterprise in the recent wonderful growth of Columbus! The East Highlands embrace 750 acres of city and suburban property, all lying within a radius of two miles of the business centre of Columbus. The first addition of this property embraces some 200 acres of level land, 100 feet above the old town, immediately adjacent to, and partly within, the city limits. This has been regularly laid off, conforming to the old town, with wide, well graded streets and avenues, all well set with shade trees. Here where but three years ago stood less than half a dozen old homes are hundreds of handsome dwellings, all occupied by a contented, happy and prosperous people. The flash of the electric light illuminates the Highlands. The postman makes his rounds and the policeman treads his beat as regularly as in the city, and every advantage that the old city has is shared here. The second, or Wildwood Park addition, embraces about 200 acres of beautifully rolling lands, higher than any territory around Columbus, except, possibly, the Alabama hills west of the city. Between this and the first addition is located Wildwood Park, containing about 100 acres of beautiful park lands, through the centre of which flows Weracoba creek, a beautiful stream of clear water, fed by perpetual springs flowing 20,000 gallons per minute, and all within a stone's throw of the Park. These grounds have been artistically laid off, and are traversed by wide drives, shaded by overhanging trees, which furnished shelter to the red man long before the sound of the steam whistle was heard echoing through the hills and dells of this beautiful Eden. Here no rattle of heavy dray or steady tramp of weary workers disturbs the quiet of this lovely spot, and as one sits under the arching vines and breathes the pure, fresh air, or wanders about amid the perfume of sweet flowers, he can scarcely realize that he is within ten minutes' ride of the busy throng that make up the business of a great and thriving city. Winding walks leading through acres of Kentucky and Texas bluegrass to rustic bridges, which span at intervals the crystal streams that thread their way through the park, singing as they ripple along the sweet hymns of nature. At night the chirp of the cricket and the song of the mocking bird lulls one to sleep. Surrounding this beautiful place are many old Southern homes, with stately columns and wide verandas, and here many of the handsome homes of the future must be erected. Already has the good work commenced, and within the past year or two quite a number of handsome modern dwellings have been built. Here the very best of society can be had, and true, old-fashioned Southern hospitality is dispensed with a liberal hand. A more cultivated, refined, hospitable people cannot be found in this beautiful South-land than those living in the East Highlands. A splendid male and female school is conducted the entire scholastic year in new buildings located in a tract of ten acres of beautifully shaded land donated to school use, and which can never be used for any other than educational purposes.

The third addition of this property, embracing several hundred acres more, is devoted to truck and dairy farms, raising all of the fruits and vegetables for which the South is fast becoming noted. Through the centre of this entire property the Columbus Railroad Company operates its belt passenger line, affording ample, cheap and rapid transportation to every portion of it. This is said to be the best built and best equipped dummy line in the South, having standard rails and cross-ties and the track ballasted with gravel. Negotiations are now pending looking to equipping this line with electricity, by which means ten minute schedules will be given to all of this property.

The policy of the company has been from the first to place before the man of moderate means a plan by which he can secure a home with the money he would pay as rent; hence they inaugurated in this city the plan of building a house and letting the purchaser pay for it on the installment plan. In purchasing a home, it is always desirable to secure a place where you can live the year round comfortably. In a well established residence community, and among refined and cultivated people, with good schools and churches, and where there is an abundance of pure water, perfect drainage and pure air; where there is no question as to who your next door neighbor will be, and where no grog-shop or other objectionable structure can be built to destroy the quiet and peace of your home; where you have electric lights and free mail delivery, police protection, cheap and rapid transportation, with absolutely correct and certain schedule, regardless of wind or weather, with comfortably heated cars in winter and open cars in summer: where property is steadily advancing in value, and where it will continue to do so, because all has been paid for cash, and the proceeds from all sales is pledged to building up, improving and developing the property; where the people who manage and control the property, and have the most interest in it,

RESIDENCE OF HON. L. F. GARRARD, EAST HIGHLANDS.

have built their own homes, and where, if they succeed, you are bound to be benefited. All of this and much more you will find on the East Highlands. The company will sell any size lot wanted. All of the lots front on wide and well graded streets, with shade trees on either side, and if you have not the means to purchase for cash, the company will aid you with cheap money on long time to help you buy and build a home.

The Georgia Midland & Gulf Railroad skirts the Northwestern portion of the Highlands for over a mile, and on this portion are many eligible sites for manufacturing plants with splendid railroad facilities. The Company will donate sufficient ground to any worthy enterprise wishing to locate here.

The Muscogee Real Estate Company, in addition to the East Highlands, own a large amount of improved and unimproved city property, which they offer at reasonable prices and on liberal terms.

To J. F. Flournoy, President and General Manager of the Company, the past great success of the work is due. He has given his energy and time to the work of making the East Highlands what it now is, the most desirable place for a home to be found. The success of the Company speaks more eloquently than any words we might write as to how well the work has been done. Mr. Flournoy, in addition to being President of the Muscogee Real Estate Company, is also President of the Columbus Investment Company and the Columbus Street Railway Company; Vice-President of the Georgia Midland & Gulf Railroad Company, Director of the Chattahoochee National Bank, and senior member of the large Cotton Commission and Warehouse firm of Flournoy & Epping. He is a man of no ordinary ability, as is evidenced by the manner in which he handles and directs the affairs of the various enterprises of which he is the executive head.

NORTH HIGHLANDS.

PROPERTY OF NORTH HIGHLANDS LAND IMPROVEMENT AND MANUFACTURING COMPANY.

Of the many alluring advantages and eminently grand and noble features which recommend Columbus as a place of residence to the capitalist, the manufacturer and the artisan, perhaps none are so highly commendable as the North Highlands addition to the city. These noble grounds, once naught but barren wilderness and woods with only nature's beauty, are now transformed by the magic arts, born of refined tastes and intelligence, into a delightful and healthful residence addition to this busy manufacturing city, teeming with many-hued flowers, striking landscapes, and scenes and surroundings the most charming that man's ingenuity and cultured knowledge can devise. To those who are as yet unfamaliar with the location we will say: The Company's property is located directly North of the city, and has an altitude of 200 feet above the highest point on the principal street in the city, and partly within the city limits, the entire area under police protection. It has a river frontage of 1900 yards, and the entire property covers an area of 335 acres, and is accessible to the city of Columbus over one of the best equipped electric railways in the South, which begins on Broad street and runs out Eleventh street to Second avenue, and out that avenue on an air line for three miles, on a twelve minutes schedule, the entire length of the property. Let fancy's eye picture a tour over this expansive addition. The broad boulevards, skirted with beautiful driveways, shaded by the green foliage of the grand line of stately trees. Then the extensive and beautiful park, embellished with striking landscapes and most charming surroundings; the view of the beautiful river with its rapids. Look where you may the view changes and fills the heart with some unexpected delight—it may be some broad expanse, arched grove, or some grotto, dell or leaf-embowered spot, a rustic bridge with blossoming vines, or a rustic fount; some rare tropical plant, flower or fern. Along carriage way, bridle path or graveled serpentine turning walks, the scene is ever changing, ever pleasing to the eye and gratifying to the taste. This property consists of 350 acres, and was purchased by the North Highlands Land Improvement and Manufacturing Company in April, 1890, the company paying for it in cash. The services of an expert landscape gardener, J. Forsyth Johnson, was secured, and the work of laying off and beautifying the property immediately began. The lots are laid off with round corners, the centre lot on the end of each block being in a triangular shape, thus avoiding the backing of any lot on the neighboring front yard. The streets are nicely graded, and a boulevard extends for 1,000 yards along the steep banks of the Chattahoochee. The scenery is beautiful. Rustic bridges cross the ravines, groves and pine trees abound, and every yard of the drive reveals some strikingly beautiful scenery: in fact, it is inspiring, and just such a place as one can come and spend months and never grow weary. A driveway is being made, twenty-five feet wide, in front of the residence property and overlooking the boulevard and the park between the boulevard and the river, and parties purchasing lots along the boulevard will be entitled to all the privileges of the club room in the large pavilion to be erected, which is free from the general pleasure-seekers at the park. For years this has been the rendezvous of the lovers of quiet and the beautiful, and now, with the rosaries to be planted around the pavilion, the beautiful drives, and many other attractive features (including bathing pools, tennis grounds, gun club grounds, etc.), it has a destiny of world-wide popularity. The lots on the boulevard have from 80 to 150 feet front, and from 140 to 250 feet depth, with twenty feet alley-way in the rear, and on the streets 50 to 150 feet depth, with ten foot alley-way. Chicago has her lake view,

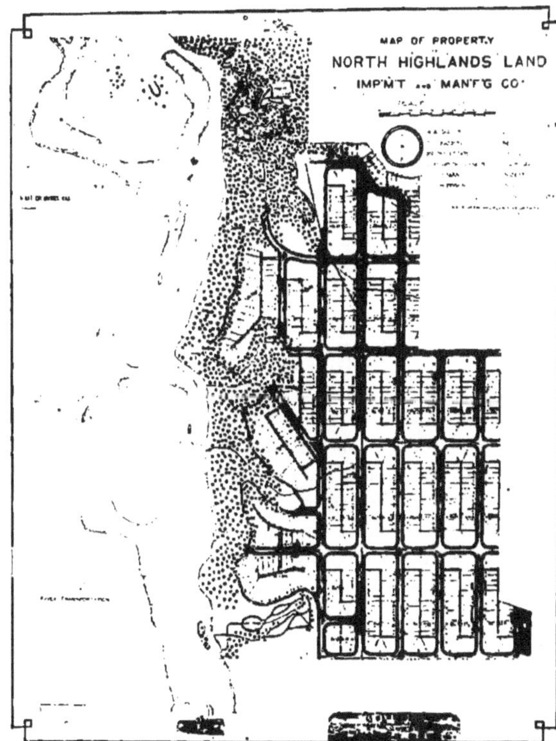

Philadelphia her Fairmount Park, Baltimore her Druid Hill Park, but in natural and rustic beauty North Highlands excels them all. Among the many views are Lovers' Leap, Sunset Rock, Marie Springs, Murmuring Falls, Eagle's Nest, and the "S" view in the river. Just above Lovers' Leap is an apparent lake, abounding in trout and other game fish.

Mr. S. A. Carter, of the firm of Carter & Bradley, one of the leading business men of the city, is President of the company: Mr. E. J. Rankin, Vice-President; Mr. J. Rhodes Browne, Secretary and Treasurer, and Messrs. J. B. Holst, D. P. Dozier, R. A. Carson and T. F. Smith, all prominent and influential citizens and business men, complete the Board of Directors. In a limited notice such as this must of necessity be, one can but give the bare facts: and we would say to those interested, volumes might be filled and then fail to carry an adequate idea; so we refrain, and simply add in conclusion: If you miss this, you miss a chance of a life-time, for this place, with its noble river and superb scenery, offers advantages unequaled anywhere in the South, and most of the eligible locations will be quickly taken up. There is no such thing as retrograding, for once let it be known and an increasing throng of both old and new guests will make it their favorite resort and stopping place.

GIRARD, ALABAMA.

TRADE, COMMERCE AND MANUFACTURING ADVANTAGES.

The growth and development of the United States stands pre-eminent among the most remarkable wonders of ancient or modern history, and yet how little our own people seem to realize its astonishing magnitude. When we stop to reflect upon the prodigious results accomplished by the nation since the close of the Revolutionary war, we are filled with amazement by the gigantic character of our own labors. In the century which has elapsed since the thirteen original States were established as a free and independent Government we have grown to a Nation of thirty-eight States and nine Territories, and fifty-six million people, having an internal commerce spread over an area three and a half million square miles, and possessed of property amounting to the enormous aggregate of forty-five thousand million dollars. These brief told facts constitute the very cone of our wonderful progress and demonstrate the unparalleled wealth of our natural resources, the unceasing industry and the boundless ambition of our people. But as the mental eye scans the grand exhibit of this one century of labor, we discover that the most astonishing features have been contributed by that portion of the country geographically defined the

SOUTH,

which has been actively progressing about one and a half score years. Within that period, however, the progress has been upon the most gigantic scale conceivable. A tour of inspection would reveal no more interesting facts concerning the giant strides of progress in this mighty South than those developed by the great State of Alabama. Among the foremost and ambitious to contribute to the fame of Alabama and aid in the general advancement of the State by properly utilizing its own quota of magnificent advantages, is the city of Girard.

It is located on the opposite bank of the Chattahoochee river from Columbus, in the corner of Russell county, which extends up to the river, the river being the line between Georgia and Alabama separating Girard from Columbus, but does not deprive it of any of the advantages of Columbus, as they have two wagon bridges, affording ample transportation.

GIRARD'S NATURAL RESOURCES.

Of first importance in considering the advantages of a city for building up the interests of commerce and manufactures are its relations to the natural resources, chief among which rank the agricultural and mineral products. To attempt the discussion of a city's resources for fostering its growth and improvement, encouraging industry and enterprise, and increasing its wealth and population without showing that it possesses favorable advantages as regards agricultural resources, is a fruitless waste of time, for without the aid of this highly important factor, none of those much desired conditions of prosperity can be expected to exist to any appreciable extent. Without doubt Alabama is one of the finest agricultural States in the Union, and as to her iron and coal she is second to none. Her soil is highly adapted to cotton, corn, oats, potatoes, fruits and vegetables, the annual average yield of each being large. Girard receives full benefit of all the transportation, banking and commercial facilities of Columbus. Although she is eminently qualified to excel as a commercial city, the principal has been to develop it as a manufacturing center. The wisdom of such endeavors is not to be questioned, since it is so plainly apparent that the city possesses in the highest degree the leading essentials for success in manufactures—endless amount of water power, comparatively no taxes, and a boundless demand for the articles after they are made, practically at our very gates, thus saving to the producers a vast sum in freights.

Skilled labor is as cheap here (as manufacturing statistics show) as in any section of the country, although the laborers realize more here because of less cost of living. Aside from the price of labor, all expenses to the manufacturer are less at this point than in any part of the South. Girard can lay claim to the title of one of the healthiest cities in the Union. The fact of the remarkably low death rate of mortality among our people has been wondered at by sanitarians, but when our conditions are carefully studied, it appears perfectly plain and satisfactory, for our city has been absolutely free from epidemics, and such contagious diseases as scarlet fever, minengitis, diphtheria, etc., are comparatively unknown. We are likewise free from the malarial influences of the river bottoms, and the few fevers we have are not of a malignant type. Our readers can see at once that Girard is the place for the manufacturer.

Rose Hill is another beautiful addition to the city, lying within the corporate limits.

Phenix City, across the river, above Girard, is a thriving town, and many of our business men live in that beautiful suburban town, and quite a number of large manufacturing establishments are also located there, because of the excellent condition of the water and the liberal inducements offered by the authorities to manufacturers seeking advantageous locations.

COLUMBUS AS A PLACE OF RESIDENCE.

From what has already been said concerning Columbus, it is plainly evident that she possesses very superior advantages for man's abiding place, constraining one almost to believe that nature especially designed the site for a residence city, leaving nothing undone that could be deemed essential to the convenience of those erecting habitations thereon. But this is an age of progress, and however perfect nature may regard its handiwork, man can always find room for improving upon it. Columbus well illustrates this inborn desire of the human race, to tear down and build over, remove and re-arrange, or tinker in some way with everything it becomes possessed of, for man has so altered, rounded up and finished her marvelously original work that few places of crudity now appear.

CLIMATE OF COLUMBUS.

Probably the most essential physical advantage of a city lies in its climate—a climate favorable to vigor of mind and health of body. The climate of Columbus, like other portions of our country, has undergone important changes within a half century. Ice is a thing that is seldom seen. Sometimes the early riser may see a thin coating of ice on the gutters, but it never remains until mid-day. Sleighing and skating hereabouts are things decidedly out of the question; in fact, the weather during January is as genial as spring. In the summer the thermometer sometimes rises for a few consecutive days above 95 degrees: but the temperature invariably diminishes sensibly after sunset, the nights being generally comfortable and refreshing, and often delightful.

HEALTHFULNESS OF COLUMBUS.

The comparative healthfulness of various cities has been made a subject of careful observation by physicians and others for more than a half century, and many cities have not even hesitated to prevaricate, to draw it mildly, concerning so serious a subject; but in all candor we assert that in a sanitary point of view Columbus is highly favored, and the tables of mortality have uniformly shown that Columbus is one of the healthiest cities in the United States.

SOCIETY OF COLUMBUS.

As would be expected all classes of society are represented here. We have in our city some of the most refined and cultivated people to be found anywhere, and unfortunately, some of whom the least that can be said is the best. No matter to what class of people one may belong, he will have no reason to echo the sad reflection of Byron: "I am among them, but not of them." All may find congenial and kindred spirits here. Upon the whole, however, no city can boast of better society than Columbus. Many of our best families descended from the earliest and most distinguished characters in the history of American independence. Identified with the city and the South from an early day, they have grown in wealth and prosperity with the growth and improvement of the country. Nor have mental culture and social refinement been neglected. For many years Columbus was noted for her institutions of learning. With all these advantages, it would be strange indeed if our best society did not reflect honor upon the city. Gentle of birth and ambitious of learning, refined by nature and hospitable to a fault, possessed of great wealth and enthusiastic lovers of art, they constitute an *ordre de monde* in which the most brilliant devotee of letters and fashion may find companionship worthy of his highest taste. All the better classes of society are liberal in their ideas, and welcome all who are worthy of their confidence and esteem. Those who have come among us in late years have been gladly received into our social circles, and many of them are now the leaders of society in wealth, culture and public spirit. Indeed, a number of our leading families—families whose recognition and hospitality would honor any guest, however high in fame or state—are those who have won their position within a recent period by their own merit and character. Thus, while our *personne de qualite* are eminently select and rigidly

VIEW OF THE RAPIDS FROM BOULEVARD, NORTH HIGHLAND.

strict in the observance of all the finer conventionalities of good society, they are generously democratic when merit knocks for admission.

CHURCHES AND RELIGIOUS INSTITUTIONS.

Columbus has always been noted for the church-going proclivities of its people, their fervid Christianity and zeal in advancing the cause of morality. The buildings are large and comfortable, are well ventilated in summer and heated in winter. All of the churches have been peculiarly fortunate in the selection of ministers, as they are all fine speakers and enjoy the highest moral and religious character. There are nineteen churches in the city, as follows: Baptists five, two white and three colored; Episcopal, one; Hebrew, one: Methodist nine, five white and four colored; Presbyterian two, one white and one colored; Roman Catholic one. The total value of church property is about $500,000, and the churches have a seating capacity for about 15,000 persons.

The limits of our book forbid our giving a more extended write-up of the churches, besides we could not obtain data from all, though we made repeated efforts.

SUNDAY-SCHOOLS.

Connected with all of the churches of the city are interesting and flourishing Sunday-schools, where many hundreds of the children and youths of the city are gathered each Sabbath day to be instructed in the great truths of the Bible, and in the religious and moral duties of life. It would be impossible to over-estimate the beneficent influence these schools have on the community. Nurseries of religion, and of virtue and good citizenship, they are justly cherished by our people as the safest guardians of their children's characters, and the surest guarantees for their future. If it is possible for the departed dead to witness the progress of human affairs, the spirit of the founder of Sunday-schools could behold no happier sight than the assemblage of all the Sunday-school children of Columbus in one grand union meeting. We are proud of our Sunday-schools, and justly so. No pains are spared by the teachers and officers, no expense withheld by the parents and churcees, to make them worthy of our city and society.

PUBLIC SCHOOLS OF COLUMBUS.

Education is the mortar that holds the social fabric together. Without it civilization would crumble to the earth. Religion itself would be lost in the Cimmerian darkness of ignorance and superstition. Pythagoras puts the necessity of education in strong language: "He that knoweth not that which he ought to know is a brute among men; he that knoweth no more than he hath need of is a man among beasts; and he that knoweth all that may be known is a god among men."

Greece, the bright, particular star in the old dark canopy of antiquity, the mother of the arts and the sciences, was first to declare the necessity of Education. Her own proud fame she owed to learning, but unfortunately for her she flourished in an age when the equality of men, the crowning glory of modern times, was unknown. She fostered Education, but the education only of her higher classes. Her common people, constituting four-fifths of her population, were left in ignorance. This was her fatal mistake. "A grievous fault it was, and grievously hath she paid it."

Education of the higher classes was carried to Rome. She, too, neglected her common people, and Rome as *Rome* is no more. A dark wave of ignorance and rapine swept over the world. All seemed to be lost. Suddenly a light flashed athwart the Western heavens, and REFORMATION stood revealed. The trumpet voice of Martin was heard proclaiming the grand truth: "Government, as the natural guardian of all the young, has the right to *compel* people to support schools. That which is necessary to the well-being of a State should be supported by those who enjoy the privileges of the State. Now, nothing is more necessary to this than the training of those who are to come after us."

Here the principle of free popular education was first proclaimed. Here it was given birth and life. Holland and Scotland hastened to apply it. Both countries claim the imperishable honor of having been first to introduce it. The result of their foresight and wisdom was, that for ages after, these nations were regarded as the most intelligent and thrifty people in Europe. Whatever they applied themselves to they excelled in. Macauley bears eloquent testimony of the race superiority of the Scotch. From Europe the principle of popular Education was brought to America; Maryland, New York, Connecticut and Massachusetts, all contend for the proud distinction of naturalizing it here. Maryland doubtless had the first free municipal schools, followed by the others in the order named, but Massachusetts was the first to adopt the State system of free schools, since adopted by all, or nearly all of the States. The Northeastern and Northern States were next to adopt it. Previous to the late war private academies were almost exclusively patronized by the people of Columbus, but at its close the uncertain condition and prospects of our citizens caused greater reliance to be placed upon the free school system.

The Columbus Public Schools were organized in 1867, and form the second oldest system of public schools in Georgia. Their growth has been steady, but constant, from their organization. The names of more than 2,400 children have been enrolled as pupils of these schools this year, and more than $26,000 appropriated for defraying the expenses of the schools for scholastic year 1891-'92. The Boys' Public School building, a most convenient, handsome school structure, costing $27,500, was finished and furnished but a little more than three years since. Since then the Chappell College property and Rose Hill school property have been bought by a generous City Council for the use of the public schools. In addition to this, there are now in the neighborhood of $20,000 in the city treasury to the credit of the school fund to be used in erecting a modern school building for the girls. Nearly two years ago a High School department was added to the primary and to the grammar departments, and is now in a most flourishing condition.

In no schools, perhaps, in the South are teachers doing more in the way of attending Normal Schools, Teachers' Institutes, etc., and in reading professional books than are the teachers of Columbus. They are intensely progressive, and the results of their teaching are exceedingly satisfactory to the patrons of the schools and the people of the city.

With a generous people to sustain them, a liberal Council to appropriate whatever funds that may be found necessary for successfully operating them, with wise, progressive trustees to direct their operations, and a superintendent and teachers thoroughly conversant with the history, principles and methods of the best school systems of the world, the Columbus Public Schools have as bright a future as any schools in the South.

CHARITABLE AND BENEVOLENT INSTITUTIONS.

"And now abideth Faith, Hope and Charity, these three; but the greatest is Charity."

Charity, the first-born of Heaven, is the divine essence within us. It is that which forms us in the image of our Maker. It is the manifestation of God himself incarnate in man. It is the lamp which lights our pathway through life and leads us on to heaven.

The mission of charity is gentleness and love. It visits the poor and consoles the friendless. It rests the weary and shelters the homeless. It feeds the hungry and clothes the destitute. It soothes the sick and comforts the sorrowing. The widow and the orphan are its wards. Its rule of life, "Love thy neighbor as thyself." Its admonition, "though I speak with the tongues of men and of angels, and have not charity, I am become sounding brass and a tinkling cymbal." In the bright galaxy of virtues, philanthrophy, benevolence, kindness, sympathy, generosity and mercy, it is the central radiant star. It is the beginning and the end of *all* virtues.

It breaks the bonds of avariciousness and selfishness, and gives with a willing and generous hand. It strives for the moral culture and elevation of mankind. It has given its apostles and evangelists, its missionaries and martyrs, its ministers and priests to humanity without money and without price. It animates the patriot and inspires the philosopher. It is the source of every generous impulse, the fountain of every noble aspiration. It is the salvation and hope of society. It is the virtue preservative of all virtues. It is the visible presence of God on earth.

The following is a list of the various charitable and benevolent and secret organizations in Columbus: Ancient Order United Workmen, two lodges; Independent Order B'nai Brith, one; Red Men, three; Knights of the Golden Rule, one; Knights of Honor, one: Knights and Ladies of Honor, one; Knights of Pythias, three; Masonic, six: National Union, two; Odd Fellows, three; Royal Arcanum, one; Typographical Union, one, and four colored secret organizations. Besides the above, Columbus has a Lodge of Elks that she may well feel proud of. It is composed of the best citizens in the town, and their devotion to protection and benevolence is observable in all the walks of life. Their motto,

> "The faults of our brothers we write upon the sands: their virtues on the tablets of love and memory."

is strictly adhered to, and could their many acts of benevolence be brought to light, a volume could be written. They have a magnificent club room, elegantly furnished and fitted up, and the latch-string is out to all visiting Elks and strangers in the city.

THE STREETS OF COLUMBUS.

"Really, the breadth of our streets, from one point of view, is to our disadvantage, as we would look more like the large city we claim to be if the streets were not so wide, and the line of buildings closer to each other. But this fault is amply compensated by the knowledge of the actual area, and the most delightful vista and openness through which circulates invigorating breezes, and much of a city's noise is lost in shady distances. Nearly every street holds a narrow strip of park, a broad space on either side for vehicles, and every available spot for a tree holds its monarch or a sturdy sapling.

BOULEVARD DRIVE—NORTH HIGHLAND

"In the centre of the city is the Court House Park, which occupies the space of an entire block, and is given over to giant trees, grassy beds bordered with flowers, winding, sanded walks, small settees, a handsome fountain presented by the Water Works Company, some tame squirrels, perambulators, nurses and children. In the centre of this stands the grim old court house, built nearly half a century ago, but its walls are so sturdy, and the exterior is so long familiar, that a sentiment clings about it, and many are loath to see it torn down. Progress decides, however, that old 'landmarks' must go, so in a few years a most commodious modern edifice will stand there."

NEWSPAPERS OF COLUMBUS.

Newspapers are the nervous system of society. They transmit intelligence to and from all parts of the body politic. Without them, or some substitute for them, public sensibility would be impossible. And as the state of the nervous system is one of the best indications of the condition of the human body, so the character of the newspapers of a community is one of the best evidences of its thrift and general intelligence.

Columbus has no reason to fear a judgment by this rule. The character of our papers is highly creditable to us as a community. We have the *Enquirer-Sun*, daily and weekly issue; *Evening Ledger*, an evening paper; *Illustrated South*, *Sunday Herald*, and *The Rifle*.

We regret that we cannot speak of them all separately, but our space will permit us to mention only one or two.

THE ENQUIRER-SUN.

The *Columbus Enquirer* was established by Mirabeau B. Lamar, in 1827. It was a weekly sheet of good size and appearance, and was edited with great ability. At that time the population of Columbus was about 1,000. Mr. Lamar severed his connection with the *Enquirer* on the first of October, 1830, and shortly removed to Texas. The paper continued under various managements, and from a weekly, in 1850, it merged into a tri-weekly. The *Daily Sun* was established on the 30th of July, 1855, by Mr. Thomas DeWolf. There were then three other papers in Columbus. There was no material change until 1873, when the *Enquirer* absorbed the *Sun*, and the paper became known as the *Enquirer-Sun*, which title it has since retained. In 1889 it passed under its present management, and since then its progress has been steady, and it is on a more solid footing and more prosperous than at any time in its career. The circulation has been largely extended; its facilities for news greatly increased, and in all departments it is fully up to the requirements of advanced journalism. It is a strong factor in the development of Columbus, and possesses great influence in the State, and its editorial columns are largely quoted from by the metropolitan journals in the North and West, of both political parties. The *Enquirer-Sun* commands the highest respect on account of its reliability, conservative and consistent course on all political measures—devoted and loyal to the Democratic party. Col. B. H. Richardson is the editor and manager, and he has gathered around him an efficient corps in the editorial and business departments.

THE EVENING LEDGER.

The *Evening Ledger* was established in 1886, by E. T. Byington & Co., and has a large and increasing circulation in Georgia and Alabama. In politics the *Ledger* is Democratic, and it has done much toward building up the city.

THE SUNDAY HERALD.

The *Sunday Herald*, edited and published by B. J. Daniel & Co., was established in 1891, and is forging ahead to a bright future. The firm consists of Messrs. B. J. Daniel, Wiley Williams, and R. F. Ellis, all of whom are old newspaper men, and the combination makes a lively team.

THE PUBLIC LIBRARY.

The Public Library is a constant source of pleasure to its large number of subscribers, and a subject of pride to all. Numbers of new books are received monthly, and the best periodicals and newspapers always at hand. The rooms, ever cheerful and inviting, are a favorite resort for the old and young of literary tastes.

The directors are untiring in their efforts to promote the welfare of this beneficent institution, in which they are ably seconded by Miss Anna Hull, the energetic and most efficient librarian.

The association confidently hopes soon to own the most elegant Library home in the South, having purchased the property of Trinity church on First avenue.

FIRE DEPARTMENT.

Columbus is also equipped with a paid Fire Department, the excellence of which is a matter of congratulation to all our citizens. As an evidence of the efficiency of the department, it may be stated that the total losses by fire, by both the property holders and insurance companies in the year 1890, was only $9,000, of which amount the property owners sustained only $1,000. The paid department has been in operation for several years, and its efficiency and trustworthiness has been thoroughly and fully demonstrated. The department is sustained by the city at an annual cost of only $15,000, which includes the wages of the firemen and all expenses of the department. The city has a fire alarm telegraph system, which has been in successful operation for a period of several years.

But our space allotted to this chapter on Columbus' advantages, is exhausted, and we must cease, though but a trifling part of the whole has been touched upon. We could fill scores more of pages about the charms of the city, found both indoors and out of doors, in its old-time houses, among the silent dead—the homes of the old age and of the new—who sleep so calmly among the beautiful surrounding of grand monuments, guardian giant trees and lovely flowers, cared for so tenderly by gentle hands and loving hearts, or amidst the innumerable fields, each with its own absorbing story, along its brooks and creeks and river, in its old relics created by limner's skillful brush and the printers' nimble type—everywhere there is an attraction that will make one linger long, and finally *long to stay*. Truly, a more delightful city than Columbus could not be desired for a place of residence. Its attractions are of the most satisfactory character to the physical, the mental and the moral demands of our nature, and in their enjoyment there most come that feeling of blissful peace that sooths so gently *only* in our own home—the dearest spot on earth.

LEADING BUSINESS HOUSES OF COLUMBUS.

We present to our readers and business community herewith a brief historical review of the prominent business houses and manufacturing firms of Columbus.

It will be interesting as an exhibit of the growth of the city for the past thirty years. The notices, as a group, embrace numbers of substantial and enterprising firms in every department of trade, including many specialties not to be obtained in any other market, and will be an assurance to those contemplating a visit for the purpose of purchasing supplies, that their every want can be fully satisfied on as favorable terms as at any point in the United States. No firm of any prominence has been willingly excluded.

1630—THE CHATTAHOOCHEE NATIONAL BANK—H. H. EPPING, PRESIDENT; E. H. EPPING, CASHIER; A. S. MASON, ASS'T CASHIER.

Banks are designed to afford safe places of deposit for money of individuals, corporations and governments, for facilitating the exchange of funds from the hands of parties who have payments to make to those who are to receive them. Thus, they are clearing houses, as it were, for the community in which they are located. They also extend aid to business men by granting loans or discounts on notes, bonds or other securities. Their origin is obscure, hidden in the unpublished and dim traditions of the past, though the merchants of Tyre Sidon and ancient Rome, it is supposed by historians, practiced some system of banking. It has come down to us through the unwritten history of cities long buried in oblivion, whose merchants transacted commerce traditionally greater than that of the present day. Banks are of three kinds, which may be classed as follows: 1st. Banks of deposit, which receive money on deposit, subject to the draft of its owner. 2d. Banks of discount, which furnish loans upon drafts, promissory notes or securities. 3d. Banks of circulation, which pay out their own notes, the credit of which is guaranteed by the general government. They are organized under an act of Congress passed in 1863, and are termed National Banks. The majority of the banks of this country at the present are of this third class, as it is considered the safest and most satisfactory method, as it combines the principle and advantages of the first and second and gives an independent circulation of its own. Among the banks acting under the last named class none in Columbus ranks higher than the Chattahoochee National Bank, No. 1630, chartered in

1865 with a capital of $100,000, and in 1885 it was re-chartered. The bank has been managed with rare financial ability and judgment, and added, by its course, materially to the financial reputation of the city, and to the facilities of her business men. We do not propose to be fulsome when we state that the management of this bank has evidenced a degree of high-toned principle and honor, and an intimate and thorough knowledge of finance as possessed by its officers, that has reflected credit not only upon themselves, but upon the city. The last statement showed a surplus of $75,000, and undivided profits, $40,000. The Directory is all that could be desired. All are men of high standing and influence in the city. The President, H. H. Epping, is a native of Germany, and came to the United States when quite young, and to Columbus in 1841, and has always been identified with the city's best interests. He is president of the following companies: The Columbus Water Works, the Alabama Connelsville Coal and Coke Company, and the Rose Hill Land Company. He possesses fine ability as a financier and business man, and is always alive to any movement that will redound to the benefit of Columbus.

Mr. A. Illges and Mr. A. Wittich are capitalists and large real estate owners; James Kyle is a large wholesale dry goods merchant; J. F. Flournoy is a member of the firm of Flournoy & Epping, cotton commission men; he is also president of the Columbus Street Railway Company, the Columbus Investment Company and the Muscogee Real Estate Company; G. P. Swift is president of the Muscogee Manufacturing Company, and one of the wealthiest men in the State; Dr. G. J. Grimes is a noted physician of the city; E. H. Epping, the cashier, is a gentleman of high social standing. Filled with push and enterprise, his aim is always to push the bank forward to the front rank of the financial institutions of the State. He is a financier in every sense of the word, and in the past has done much for the bank.

CARTER & BRADLEY—Fontaine Warehouse, Cotton Factors and Commission Merchants.

In dilating at length, and in detail upon the industrial advantages of this city, it must not be forgotten that they arise, to a large extent, from a fortuitous geographical position, a climate unusually equable, and magnificent water facilities, which place it in direct communication with the finest cotton growing district in the world. These considerations have exerted a vital influence in promoting the cotton trade, which is here carried on upon a scale the magnitude of which cannot be readily appreciated without carefully reviewing the trade in detail.

In undertaking such a work, we shall begin with reference to the enterprise of Carter & Bradley, which was established in 1885, and who are to-day doing a large and profitable business, handling from 18,000 to 20,000 bales of cotton per annum. Eighteen men are required to conduct this business, the pay-roll amounting to $200 per week. They carry an average number of 3,000 bales in stock, and are continually receiving and shipping the staple, consignments coming from this State, Alabama and Florida; a large portion of their business coming from the lower river country in the Chattahoochee Valley—a section of country that is fertile, and productive of good staple and large crops, which are transported to this market by packet. The individual members of the firm are S. A. Carter and W. C. Bradley, both young men, and well known as business men with unimpeachable reputations for honorable, upright and liberal dealings, and as a firm, they are justly entitled to the esteem and confidence of the general public. Always active in everything that tends to the advancement of the commerce of our city, they are respected by their associates in trade as well as by the large number of customers they have secured by their intelligent efforts and liberal dealings. It may be judged that this firm is composed of brainy men, when it is shown that the positions they hold in other enterprises are of great importance. Mr. Carter holds the position of President of the Columbus Grocery Company, is President of the North Highland Railroad Company; he is also a Director in the National Bank of Columbus, and in the Georgia Home Insurance Company.

Mr. Bradley is Vice-President of the Columbus Grocery Company, a Director in both the Third National Bank, and the Columbus Savings Bank, and a member of the Board of Trade.

Mr. Bradley was born at Oswichee, Ala., June 28, 1863. He located in Columbus in 1884. The firm of Carter & Bradley is widely known in this section, and their spacious warehouse of 210x160 feet, situated on Front street, presents a business-like appearance, with its side-tracks to the front, to the rear and inside, where cars are being loaded and unloaded with their burdens of the fleecy staple.

M. SELIGMAN—Clothing, Hats, Boots and Shoes, 22 Front Street.

Of the several firms in this city engaged in the clothing trade, none are better stocked, or conducted with a more thorough knowledge of the requirements of the trade, than the establishment of M. Seligman. He came to Columbus in 1885, with comparatively no capital, and opened up business for his father, and with his sterling business qualities, energy and push, he soon built up such an enormous trade that he was compelled to open another store at 1019 Broad street, to accommodate his customers; and still his trade continued to increase, and he opened up another store at 1226 Broad, and successfully managed the three stores till May, 1891, when he beceme sole proprietor of the store at 22 Front street, where he still does an overwhelming business. Mr. Seligman deserves much credit for the skilled and successful manner in which he managed the three stores. He carries a complete stock of men's, boy's and children's clothing, gent's furnishing goods of every description, hats, caps, trunks, valises, etc. His prices are the lowest. A visit to his busy establishment will convince you that he sells goods cheaper than any house in the city. He is a native Russian Jew, possessing fine business qualities; came to this country in 1883, and to Columbus in 1885, and his success in business has been remarkable. We commend our readers to the establishment of M. Seligman.

R. G. DUN & CO.—MERCANTILE AGENCY, 1137½ BROAD STREET, J. J. MOBLEY, MANAGER.

The importance of the line of business carried on by Messrs. R. G. Dun & Co. can scarcely be estimated, so vast are its ramifications and so important are its bearings upon the trade of every city. By means of the information which they afford to their subscribers, many of whom are saved heavy losses, and unreliable and unscrupulous dealers or merchants are made known to the community. The Columbus branch was started January 1, 1890, with J. J. Mobley, Manager. They have taken here, as elsewhere, a front rank and outrank all other agencies in number of subscribers, and this fact is due to the energy and business capacity of Mr. Mobley and his assistant, Mr. I. P. Clark, a young man of marked ability, and also to the exactness of their reports, that come from all parts of the Union and Canada. R. G. Dun & Co. have been doing business since 1841, and now covers the American continent and Europe. They have 150 branch offices. and are considered by far the best agency. The Columbus office covers seventeen counties in Georgia in a manner characteristic of the Company. Mr. Mobley is a native of Georgia, and has been in the employ o f the agency for some years. Under his supervision the business is increasing rapidly. He is a member of the Columbus Board of Trade, and is a gentleman of excellent standing and marked business capacity.

THE HOWARD SHOE STORE H. M. & M. W. HOWARD, PROPR'S, 1112 BROAD STREET.

The design of our volume being to diffuse general information concerning the industries and resources of Columbus, we would be doing an injustice to one of the best firms in the city, to neglect passing mention of the proprietors of The Howard Shoe Store. This house, though not possessing the same claim to antiquity as some of its contemporaries, is, nevertheless, ranked as a leading establishment in the boot and shoe trade of this city. This enterprise was started in 1880, by Mr. Wm. Meyers, the present proprietors succeeding to the business in 1891. Possessing ample capital, they have, by judicious management and strict attention to business, secured a large and lucrative trade in Georgia and Alabama, particularly in those portions lying contiguous to Columbus. They carry a stock of $10,000 worth of goods, made by the best manufacturers of the country, and the annual transactions will reach $20,000. The premises occupied are 30x100 feet in size, and the display of goods is both artistic and satisfactory. Prompt and courteous attention is paid to all customers, two assistants being employed, and both proprietors giving personal attention to the trade.

Messrs. H. M. and M. W. Howard are the individual members of the firm, both natives of our city. Mr. H. M. Howard was born here in 1843, Mr. M. W.

Howard in 1864; both active, energetic business men, who are pushing the busi- to its greatest limits. Mr. M. W. Howard has been engaged in this branch of trade since 1883, and in assuming control of this well-known concern has infused new life into its management. The success which has already attended this enterprise is such as to warrant the prediction that the house will, ere long, rank first among similar institutions of the city.

THOS. S. MITCHELL, M. D.—Resident Physician and Surgeon, Office 1141 Broad Street.

A work of this kind would not be complete without the names of some of our most prominent physicians, and none rank higher in the medical fraternity of our city than Dr. Mitchell. He is a man of much experience, both as a physician and surgeon, graduating twice, first in 1854, and again in 1866. As an evidence of the public appreciation of his qualities as a physician and public spirited citizen, Dr. Mitchell has been selected to hold positions of honor, trust, and confidence; practicing as surgeon two years in the United States army, also city physician of Columbus for six years. Dr. Mitchell is a native Alabamian; he practiced for twenty-seven consecutive years in Hamilton, Ga., and now enjoys a large practice in Columbus and adjoining counties.

SWIFT MANUFACTURING COMPANY—Plaids, Cottonades, Ticking, Stripes, etc., Improved Mitcheline Bed Spreads.

Columbus has, during the last decade, manifested more spirit of progress and enterprise than at any other period of her history. Evidences of substantial prosperity are becoming abundant, and industry, the hand-maid of civilization, is exercising her potent influence. Manufactories of staples are springing into existence, one of the surest harbingers of an awakening to the enterprise that is elsewhere characterizing this progressive age. In the history of cities, from the days of Tyre and Thebes, the first stimulus towards prosperity has been from the building of manufactories, and in modern times, no city has become truly great and metropolitan that has not encouraged manufacturing. The great cotton interests of this section demand certain classes of goods which every kindred interest would suggest, could be produced here to a greater advantage than by importing them from Northern marts.

The Swift Manufacturing Company, an institution of conspicuous magnitude, was chartered in November, 1882, by Geo. P. Swift, Sr., Geo. P. Swift, Jr., W. A. Swift, Louis Hamberger and G. M. Williams, capitalized at $200,000. In 1883 the mills were erected, and a complete outfit of the most improved machinery put in, and they at once began an active and profitable business, placing their products throughout the Southern States, and many of them in the Northern markets. Mr. G. M. Williams is President and general manager, and Mr. Sam Salisbury Secretary and Treasurer, and under the guidance of these practical business men, the institution is kept in a most healthy state of prosperity. Four hundred hands are here given employment, which requires a monthly pay-roll of $8,000. There are 10,000 spindles and 450 looms busily clattering away, turning out plaids, cottonades, ticking, stripes, and the celebrated Mitcheline Bed Spreads, which are produced in various tints and most beautiful designs. This company has sold enormous quantities of these spreads in all parts of the United States. It so happened that, among the number of hands brought here from England, there was a weaver named Mitchell, who had perfected the system of weaving this peculiar style of bed spread, and from whence came the name, "Mitcheline Bed Spreads," the manufacture and sales of which have been a most flattering success.

The out-put of this company is $350,000 worth of goods per annum. Great credit is due the officers for the enterprise and ability they have displayed in developing this branch of industry and carrying it to its present successful position, contributing materially to the reputation of the city, and stimulating enterprise by their example.

COLUMBUS GROCERY COMPANY - JOBBERS OF STAPLE GROCERIES, 1037 TO 1045 FRONT STREET.

In all our prominent towns and cities, there are always those whose energies and business abilities qualify them for leaders in business pursuits, and in whatever occupation they are engaged, they will be found to excel in excellence of stock, and in ability to meet the requirements of their trade. As an important branch of the commercial industries of Columbus, the grocery business is entitled to a large share of consideration, and in this connection we direct attention to the wholesale establishment of the Columbus Grocery Company, situated on Front street, from No. 1037 to 1045, and running back 160 feet, three stories high. The stock embraces the fullest and most complete line of groceries and articles pertaining to the trade to be found in the city, including both staple and fancy groceries and provisions, canned goods, foreign and domestic fruits and nuts, wooden and willow ware, confectioneries, choice tobaccos and cigars, notions, etc. The stock is constantly being replenished by fresh arrivals from producers, manufacturers and jobbers: a flattering patronage from the States of Georgia, Alabama and Florida having been enjoyed since the establishment of the business. The Columbus Grocery Company was incorporated July 1, 1891, with S. A. Carter, President; W. C. Bradley, Vice-President; and C. E. Caverly, Secretary and Treasurer, and a stronger quota of officials it would have been difficult to have secured. Each one of these gentlemen is now classed among the leading business men of Columbus, they having shown themselves to be composed of that material which tends to build an industrial city into one of prominence.

Mr. S. A. Carter was born at Florence, Ga., March 4, 1854. He removed to Columbus in 1884, when he became associated with Mr. W. C. Bradley, in the warehouse and commission business. In 1891, Mr. Carter was instrumental in organizing the North Highland Land Improvement and Railroad Company, which enterprise is one of the attractions of Columbus. Mr. Carter is also a Director in the National Bank of Columbus, and the Georgia Home insurance Company. Mr. W. C. Bradley, the Vice-President of the Columbus Grocery Company, was born at Oswichee, Ala., June 28, 1863. He located here eight years ago, when he entered the business in which he is now engaged, and although a comparatively young man, it has been demonstrated that he has an old head on him, adopting and carrying out a sound and safe policy in the management of affairs in which he is interested; this being evident from the fact that his counsel is required in the Directory of the Third National Bank, and the Columbus Savings Bank, and also, as a member of the Board of Trade of this city. Mr. Bradley is ever on the alert to lend his aid to any undertaking looking to the advancement of the city and the public interests of the citizens of Columbus. Mr. C. E. Caverly, the Secretary and Treasurer, was born in Newport, Fla., September 22, 1852. He began the study of the grocery business in 1875, since which time he has continued to give it his close attention, until to-day he is looked upon as a thoroughly posted grocery man, second to none in the country, and it is his work that is doing so much towards bringing Columbus to the front as a grocery market, which fact, within itself, is of much value to the mercantile reputation of the city.

The Columbus Grocery Company was organized with a paid-up capital of $50,000, the average amount of stock carried being from $15,000 to $25,000, and the annual business $500,000. Sixteen men are required to attend to the immense business of this enterprise, and special attention is given to filling and shipping orders received from a distance. Every facility for handling groceries has been arranged, side tracks being on three sides of the building, thus enabling cars to be loaded and unloaded at the doors. Directing attention to the manner in which it is conducted, the amplitude of its resources and facilities, and remarking that, as ranking first among its contemporaries, the establishment is of that class which commands the respect, confidence and consideration of the city at large.

FLOURNOY & EPPING—Warehouse and Commission Merchants, Twelfth and Front Streets.

Through a wise provision of nature, the different sections of this vast country have each some commercial function or element which exerts a controlling influence on trade. This condition is brought about by divers causes—geographical position and natural mineral deposits are most important, while in some localities facilities for transportation, and the fecundity of the soil for producing cereals, are the basis on which ultimate wealth and commercial prosperity have their foundation. The West has her great grain products and unequaled facilities for transportation; the middle tier of States have their invaluable coal and iron resources; this part, the South, has, to a certain extent, a unification of all these elements of progress, furnished by nature with a prolific hand, only awaiting development by enterprise. These are cotton, the king of vegetable products, and the wonderful deposits of coal and iron underlying the whole section, and last, and of equal importance, our splendid facilities for transportation, both water and rail. This is particularly true of this section of Georgia. The city of Columbus receives yearly about 90,000 bales of cotton, and it is but natural that we should find the live, progressive business men of the city engaged in handling the fleecy staple.

The most extensive commission men in our market are Flournoy & Epping. The firm, composed of John F. Flournoy, and H. H. Epping, jr.; was started in 1873 by Flournoy, McGehee & Co., and changed in 1877 to Flournoy & Epping. They have a large capital, and no interior house in the South enjoys a better reputation than this. They handle about 20,000 bales yearly. Both members of the firm are largely identified with Columbus and her progress, and are heavy real estate owners. Mr. Flourney is President of the following Companies: Columbus Railroad Company, Columbus Investment Company, Muscogee Real Estate Company; Vice-President Georgia Midland and Gulf Railroad, Director Chattahoochee National Bank. Mr. Epping is a man of public spirit, pushing and energetic. In 1884 he was elected Alderman, which office he held with dignity and respect, and honor both to himself and the city.

GEORGE O. BERRY—STEAM BRICK MANUFACTURER; ANY STYLE OF BRICK OR TILING MADE TO ORDER.

The condition of raw material is an item that is of much concern to the manufacturer—superiority of grade produces an increased value to the product. The abundance of material to be found at this point for the manufacture of brick is peculiarly superior to that to be found at any other place in this section of the country, which fact brought forth a remark from a contractor in Albany, who said that "God must have favored Columbus when he made material for making brick." Hence, it is, that this city has ever been noted for the manufacture of superior brick. The pioneer in this industry was W. W. Berry, who came South from Wheeling W. Va., in 1845, and shortly thereafter began moulding brick for the local market, and continued in the business the balance of his life.

Mr. George O. Berry, the subject of this sketch, is the son of W. W. Berry. He was born in Eufaula, Ala., in 1847, coming to Columbus in 1850 with his father. Here he was raised and brought up in the business, thereby gaining a thorough knowledge of this industry. Mr. Berry owns seventy-six acres of ground, upon which is to be found the finest brick material, thereby giving him an inexhaustible supply. Mr. Berry is furthermore fully equipped with the latest improved machinery, among which is to be seen the "Penfield," "Plunger," "Frey-Seckler Company Auger," and "H. Brewer" brick machines; also, three engines and boilers, two twenty-five horse-power and one ten horse-power. He is operating four plants—two machine and two hand—this large outfit giving a capacity of 100,000 brick per day, the output being composed of pressed brick, common brick, ornamental brick and tiling. Mr. Berry's establishment is situated southeast from the jail, at the junction of the Central, Columbus Southern and Georgia Midland and Gulf railroads. Each of these roads secure hauls from him, transporting his product north, east, south and west, going into the States of Georgia, Alabama, and Florida. Some of his most extensive shipments go to the eastern part of the State, including Savannah and Brunswick. Thoroughly identified with the progressive spirit of this city, and possessed of the essential requisites of sound judgment and care of his business policy, he presents the strongest claims to popular favor with those desiring business relations in this department of our business activities.

JONES BROTHERS—Sash, Doors and Blinds, Lumber, Contractors.

Statistics show that out of every hundred men who embark in business, ninety-seven meet with failure, while only three succeed in driving their business through to a successful termination. We take pleasure in referring to the firm of Jones Brothers as successful business men. They began business in Columbus in the fall of 1888, with small capital, but as their business increased, they added

more machinery, and erected more buildings, and so continued until to-day their plant comprises two acres of ground, nearly half of which is covered with buildings equipped with the very best and latest improved wood-working machinery which is driven by a 100-horse power engine; and they make any and every thing that can be manufactured of wood. Among the employees are to be found some of the most skillful artisans and experts in the various departments of the business. An inspection of their warehouse will show a complete stock of sash, doors, blinds, lime, plaster, cement, paints and oil, and everything needed in the building line. In their work-shops are to be found a full assortment of patterns and designs for brackets, scroll work, draperies, newells, ballusters, and all other ornamental wood work, with machinery and mechanics ready to turn anything in a finished style and on short notice. On the yards are to be seen towering stacks of all kinds of lumber, laths and shingles, and the facilities are such that they can fill any kind of an order for material to build anything from a chicken-coop to a steamboat, figuratively speaking. The success of this firm has been phenominal, and although in business for the short space of three and a half years, their reputation has gone abroad beyond the limits of Georgia and adjoining States, and orders are received for lumber in car-load lots from distant sections, even as far off as Rhode Island. Messrs. Jones Brothers are young men, and are wide awake to the requirements of an energetic and practical business policy.

Mr. Rufus Jones, the senior member of the firm, is now, and has been from the beginning, the general manager, and to his close attention, untiring energy, watchful care and skillful management, the phenominal success of this young firm is chiefly due; and while their business career is not yet ended, either in failure or success, we feel confident that when that period is reached, Columbus will add the name of Jones Brothers to her list of successful men, of whom she has her full quota of the three per cent who never fail.

CHATTAHOOCHEE BREWING COMPANY—Office 1205 Broad Street Capital $250,000.

A one-horse wagon, on which were two men, drove into Columbus, Ga., one bright spring day in the year 1887. These two persons were brewers from Walhalla, S. C., a German settlement, where, after failing to make the success their ambition deserved, were prospecting for a more profitable field. An iron kettle, capable of brewing one and one-half barrels of beer at a time, and three ordinary wine butts in which to ferment, age, and store it after brewing, comprised, with their wagon and horse, their stock in trade. They took a great fancy to Columbus, so much so indeed that they determined to make it their stopping place, but after having had a careful analysis made of the water, they discovered that it was not very good for brewing purposes, but just across the river, in Alabama, they found an inexhaustible supply having all the natural constituents necessary for the brewing of the finest beer. Having shown, in a small way, the excellent beverage that could be made with it, they interested a few of the most prominent citizens, forming a company which finally, from the investment of a few hundred dollars, have at last created a company whose vested interests in the Brewery now amount to $250,000. Daily the fame of its production increases, and with its popularity, the sales go upward, and with the rapid strides made by the Chattahoochee Brewing Company, it will soon be among the most prosperous in the entire Southern States. The Directors are the leading business men of Columbus, and characteristic of their enterprising spirit, they decided at the annual meeting of 1891, to have the quality of the beverage made equal to any beer in the world, regardless of expense and work. Deeming this course a sound policy, they proceeded at once to put it in operation, and forthwith opened communications with Mr. E. M. Walsh, of Dublin, Ireland, a man with wide experience in the brewing business, and possessed of great ability as a manager, who will, under no circumstances, allow any beer to be taken out of the brewery that is not perfectly brewed and carrying the proper age; and, adhering to the policy of making the best beer, the finest German hops and best American malt in the market is used. Mr. Walsh will not have any cereoline, rice, grape sugar, glucose, or acids of any kind put in the product, and guarantees that it will stand a chemical test with any beer in the United States, and as a health tonic, is unsurpassed by any beverage whatever; and last, but not least, possesses a flavor highly pleasing to the most fastidious. The brewery has an outfit of the latest improved machinery, including ice machines, Corless engines, compression ice and ammonia machines. Thirty hands are given employment, among which are skilled brewers from Germany. The officers are: E. H. Epping, President; E. M. Walsh, Vice-President and General Manager; C. A. Epping, Secretary and Treasurer. The product of this industry is shipped largely throughout Georgia, Florida and Alabama, and is sold in every bar in Columbus, both in bottles and kegs. The Chattahoochee Brewing Company will do much towards bringing Columbus prominently to the front as an enterprising manufacturing city.

J. B. HARRISON & CO.—Real Estate, Stock and Bond Brokers, Twelfth Street, Near Broad.

The leading real estate dealers in our city is J. B. Harrison & Co. The business of this firm is under the personal charge of Mr. Harrison, a man of marked ability and high business honor, a person above all others to take charge of a business of this kind, and he will always be found to be a gentleman in whom confidence can be placed. The other members of the firm are John F. Flournoy, a real estate man of note, who is doing much to advance the various interests of the city, and H. H. Epping, a gentleman of high standing in the community, who is identified with the progress and development of our city. This firm has much valuable city propery on their books, both improved and unimproved, of which they will gladly give any desired information. The firm of J. B. Harrison & Co. commends *itself* to the public as one from whom the most liberal treatment may be expected.

T. S. SPEAR—Watchmaker and Jeweler, and Dealer in Fine Diamonds, Watches, Clocks, Jewelry, Silver and Silver-Plated Ware, 1121 Broad Street.

Columbus has in every department of trade stores equal to any to be found elsewhere, and of no line is this more true than of jewelry. Each store seems to vie with the other in the beauty and display of their exhibits, and among these the handsome store of T. S. Spear holds a leading place, both for the elegance of the line carried, but particularly for the fine work done in the watch repairing and special departments.

Mr Spear was born in New Jersey, Jan. 19, 1825, but early in life moved to Charleston, S. C., where he learned his trade, in which he has no superior. He followed the business in Charleston for several years in connection with his brother J. E. Spear, prior to 1857, in that year coming to Columbus and buying out L. B. Purple. He had in cash capital about $15,000, and having push, energy and a determination to succeed, he quickly won for himself a high position. Backed by high business honor, he determined to turn out only work that would prove satisfactory alike to himself and his patrons. Mr. Spear is identified with the progress of the city, and her best interests are always first in his mind. He has served as Alderman, filling the office with that same spirit of honesty and uprightness that is characteristic of the man. During the war the store was robbed of a large stock of costly diamonds by Gen. Wilson's raiders. Mr. Spear is an optician of no mean skill. He carries a large stock of glasses, in which he does the largest business in this section.

S. L. SIMMONS—MEAT MARKET, 16 TENTH STREET.

Among the enterprises most essential to the well being of the people of a city, none are more important than those which furnish the daily supply of provisions. Among this class we cheerfully devote space to the meat market of Mr. S. L. Simmons. The fresh meats sold by this house are always the choicest, as Mr. Simmons does not handle any but stall-fed meat. It has long since been demonstrated that grass-fed beef does not have the tender, juicy taste that the stall-fed meat has, hence the stall-fed meat has the lead. The sausage put up by Mr. Simmons cannot be surpassed in quality. His premises numbering 16 Tenth street, occupies 25x60 feet, affording ample room for his sausage-making machinery, and all appliances necessary to the successful conduct of his business. He also runs stall No. 7 in the market house. Mr. Simmons was born in Macon County, Ala., and came to Columbus in 1880: was employed by Cook & O'Brien to work in their market, where he served two years, then, with D. L. Thomas, five years, and then entering business for himself. Five years has built up a trade second to none. Mr. Simmons has followed his trade for twelve years, and no one better understands its details or the wants of his customers than he. He is a man of high integrity and sterling business qualities, attentive and courteous to all his patrons, liberal and conscientious in all his dealings, he richly merits the success he has attained.

R. JEFFERSON—GROCERIES, 1041 BROAD STREET.

In a history of the advance and development of Columbus, with reference to commercial affairs, the grocery trade must always occupy a very prominent position as a branch of mercantile industry, contributing is no small degree to the present commercial importance of the city. Among those houses whose extended transactions and high standing entitles them to special mention, is that of Mr. R. Jefferson, being one of the largest establishments in the city. Mr. Jefferson occupies the building located at No. 1041 Broad street, 35x137 feet in size, where he has stored a complete stock of the choisest staple and fancy groceries, reaching $10,000 in value. Four assistants are employed, and the annual transactions will reach $65,000.

Mr. Jefferson conducts business with a capital of $25,000, and is interested in an invention of his own make, which has become very popular with all the farmers who have met with it. This is Jefferson's celebrated Plow Fender. This Fender is a wonder to the farmer, saving time and quality in work to the ploughman in any kind of crop, cotton, corn, vegetables, etc., and its cheapness puts it in reach of every one. Price, one dollar, while it saves ten dollars, under guarantee. The out-put the first year was 3,000, and they are highly recommended by each purchaser. Mr. Jefferson was born here in 1849, and is well known in business circles as a gentleman of large business abilities. His transactions are large throughout Georgia, Alabama and Florida. He is justly esteemed for those attributes which invariably lead to success.

THE COLUMBUS BARREL MANUFACTURING COMPANY—Works, Opposite Central Railroad Compress.

For wood-working establishments it is evidenced that Columbus has an admirable situation. From the large industries now in operation here, and among the most prominent, is to be found the Columbus Barrel Manufacturing Company, the only one of the kind in this part of the South, and one of the most extensive in the entire country, their output being 150 barrels daily. These are used for oil, spirits of turpentine, cidar and vinegar, and are shipped to points throughout the States of Georgia, Alabama and Florida, and besides barrels, this company deals in staves, headings, kegs, etc. Seventy hands are here given employment. Steam power is used, a fifty horse-power engine is required to drive the machinery, the very latest improvements in machinery is included in the outfit, enabling them to lower the cost of production to a considerable extent, and one feature is conspicuous, which is, the superior grade of the Columbus-made barrels and kegs. The shipping facilities are fine, as they have side-track connection with every railroad centering in Columbus. The officers of the company are: M. M. Hirsch, President, and H. Elson, Manager, both residents of this city, and are classed among the most enterprising business men of Columbus. The business was established seven years ago, and by good management and a straightforward business policy, they have steadily increased their trade every year, until now the business reaches $100,000 per annum. The size of the grounds is just one acre, covered with buildings and material. The weekly pay roll is $350. Columbus is justly proud of this industry, which demonstrates to the outside world that she is a desirable point for manufactures.

THE EAGLE CLOTHING MANUFACTURING COMPANY—Opposite Eagle and Phenix Mills.

In noting the improvements of the New South and the varied industries springing up, that of the manufacturing of jeans pants has grown quite prominent. During the past few years a new departure has taken place in the woolen jeans and cottonades consumption, inasmuch as the retail merchant, who, formerly purchased regularly every year, a stock of jeans and cottonades in the piece, but now, instead, he buys ready-made pants of these materials, his customers prefering the ready-made garments, as they are more regularly put together than can be done at home, and is just as low in the cost, if not cheapear, hence, the increased demand for pants in the South among the farmers, miners and mechanics, and from the fact that the 60,000 spindles in Columbus produced the material for making pants, was a sufficient inducement to a party of enterprising men of our city to organize a pants factory, to be called the Eagle Clothing Manufacturing Company, with M. L. Patterson, President: Abe Strauss, Secretary and Treasurer, and L. Meyer, Manager. This company, though but a few years in the trade, has gained a reputation on the merits of the work sent out, and one feature of their make is the strong seams and special patterns. Their pants and overalls are made from jeans, cottonades, denims, etc., that are manufactured specially for them. It is only necessary to select a particular pattern and name the weight and material and place their order with some of the cotton and woolen manufacturers here and thus the exact goods needed are made. The Eagle pants are well made and are sold to meet any competition, from any market, and this is one other industry assisting in bringing Columbus to the front as a manufacturing city.

DELMONICO RESTAURANT—H. A. PAYNE, PROP., 1021 BROAD STREET, OPPOSITE CENTRAL HOTEL.

The popular and fertile section, of which Columbus is the center, gives her great importance as a point of distribution for all kinds of supplies. To persons visiting the city on purchasing tours, or for pleasure, it will be interesting to know that the city contains a number of establishments designed for the comfort and convenience of guests. No restaurant in the city is better prepared for the entertainment of patrons, or furnishes a table that, for cleanliness, excellence in cooking, and the season's luxuries than the "Delmonico." A still greater advantage is in having at its head Mr. H. A. Payne, an experienced caterer, whose qualifications as a host are excelled by none; frank, genial and with true ideas of hospitality, he gives to the restaurant more varied and greater advantages than can be enjoyed elsewhere. He and his employees are courteous and obliging to the patrons of his establishment, and everything is prepared in a way that will meet the wishes of the most fastidious. The restaurant is run on the European plan, meals are furnished table *d'hote*, or *a la carte*, and can be had day or night. Mr. Payne has constantly on hand all the delicacies of the season, which are served in excellent style. This is the chief restaurant in the city that caters to ladies patronage. Ice cream parlors are attached, in which all the popular ices are served.

MILLER & MILLER—

Two brothers, T. T. Miller and B. S. Miller, compose the above firm. They are both young men, born and reared in a neighboring county, in the noted little town of Buena Vista. Although identified with Columbus from their early childhood, they did not locate here until August 1, 1890. Since that time, by their pluck, their skill and merit, they have established for themselves an enviable reputation, and are recognized lawyers of ability, enjoying a lucrative practice. One among the first steps of progress made by this firm was the purchase of a library, at a cost of $2,500, and not only is it said to be well selected, but is acknowledged to be one of the finest libraries in the city. This makes a fine showing in their behalf, for, although they may never be looked upon only from the outside, they give to their office and their surroundings an appearance, a dignity, a learning that can in no wise be claimed by the young practitioner who seats himself in an office with no furniture but one chair and a table, and no tools but the Georgia code and a form book. The firm of Miller & Miller is a permanent institution. They have become thoroughly identified with the city, and whether for weal or for woe, their fortunes are cast among Columbus people, whose destiny shall be their destiny, whose future shall be their future. The welfare of the city they have thoroughly at heart, and all schemes of public enterprise, in all efforts to advance her material progress and to add to her future glory, they'll be found enthusiastic supporters and advocates. Since their location here, the business of Miller & Miller has been largely in excess of their expectations, for, within about eighteen months' time, they have become the regular retained attorneys of some of the most important corporations and largest wholesale houses in the city. Close application to business, living in your office during office hours, promptness and reliability, merits success any and everywhere, and these are the elements most conspicuous with the young men. Mr. B. S. Miller, the junior member, is a graduate of the Lumpkin Law School, of the University of Georgia. We take pleasure in commending them to our readers, both home and abroad, as prompt, reliable, energetic and capable attorneys.

J. K. ORR & CO.—Manufacturers and Wholesale Dealers in Reliable Boots and Shoes.

Columbus a wholesale shoe market! and one of prominence; it equals the most extensive Eastern markets as regards prices, grades, terms, rates, etc., and this fact brought about by the efforts of one man, who is at the head of the wide awake establishment of J. K. Orr & Co. This business was instituted in 1884, and although young, has gained a reputation that insures for it at extensive trade. From the first year of its life this house has sprung forward with a bound and entered the race for trade that has rewarded it with a first prize. Keeping well up and in advance of their many competitors, they have placed goods with highly satisfactory results in the States of Georgia, Alabama, Mississippi and Florida, and are annually reaching out and adding new buyers to their large list. Mr. Orr, who has the management of affairs, came to Columbus nineteen years ago from New York city, and entered the establishment of J. Kyle & Co., and being possessed of an unusual amount of energy and skill, he was placed at the head of the wholesale shoe department, and in 1884 organized the present firm, and so thorough is his knowledge of the wants of the Southern trade in the shoe line, that he has rapidly grown in favor as a shoe merchant with this section, where his lines are so largely used. The business has grown from a small trade to an annual business of over half a million dollars. Mr. Orr begun the study of the shoe business when a youth, and by close application brought himself up to a high standard as a shoe man, and after locating in the South, acquainted himself with the demands of the Southern trade, which is totally different from that of the Western and Eastern, hence his superior capability for filling the wants of this section. J. K. Orr & Co. represent a dozen of the best factories of the East; their goods are all made to order, and are sold from Columbus at the same prices as are named by their Boston house. With ample capital, long experience and superior management, the firm of J. K. Orr & Co. are instrumental in gaining for Columbus the reputation of being a shoe market second to none in the South, and one that is a pride to the city of Columbus.

BRUSH ELECTRIC LIGHT AND POWER COMPANY.

Mr. W. A. Swift was the first citizen to take steps towards having Columbus adopt a system of electric lights for the streets, but at first his efforts were not encouraged, from the fact that the city government was part owner of the gas company, and it required some time in which to gain public favor for the substitution of electric lights, which was finally done, when the organization of this company was perfected, and during the past few years they have taken advantage of every improvement on this wonderful discovery, and to-day are thoroughly equipped for furnishing lights and power. The officers are: W. R. Brown, President: W. A. Swift, Secretary and Treasurer: and W. E. Boileau, Superintendent. Mr. Brown is the Chief officer of the Columbus Iron Works. Mr. Swift is one of the most prominent business men of Columbus: he is also President of the Paragon Manufacturing Company, and Secretary of the Muscogee Manufacturing Company, and is also a city Alderman, representing the Fourth ward. Mr. Boileau, although a citizen of Columbus but three years, has become identified as one of our most active and progressive business men. He is an expert electrician, and spares no pains to keep the system in thorough working order. One hundred and fifty arc and 3,000 incandescent lights are used. The company is making a specialty of lighting up residences, and now have more than 1,000 lights in this department. It has recently been necessary to add more power, and now the spacious brick building contains two engines of 150 horse power each, and one of 300 horse power: two boilers of 125 horse power each, and two of 150 horse power—a total of 550 horse power for the boilers and 600 for the engines. The lights furnished by this machinery are as perfect as can be made, giving entire satisfaction to patrons.

G. J. PEACOCK—Clothing Manufacturer, No. 1200 Broad Street.

Some sniviling, cynical, threadbare philosopher, poet, nondescript, or what not, once upon a time gave existence to the maxim, aphorism, proverb or axiom, "Clothes do not make the man." Pardon us, gentle reader, if we disagree with such a notion. John Ruskin, one of the most pleasing writers of the world of modern literature, made use of the expression, "Show me a man's books and I will read you his character," and the same is true when applied to the outer garments of our fellow man. Clothes certainly do not *make* the man, but clothes are indicative of the man, and we rate our opinion of strangers just as we see them habited. The subject is one that has been discussed and meditated over ever since the days when Adam was content to pick posies in company with Eve, and she to while away the hours, even in Paradise, made their "garments of fig leaves." This commendable taste or habit has been thus handed down to us by our first parents, and year by year some new design springs up, some handsome fashion that, despite the fallen condition of humanity, causes us to revere the memory of our common primogenitor, and to accept our discomfiture *cum grano salis*. Each new season brings to us new adaptations, made to beautify and adorn the figure, as well as for utilities sake. This trade, then, having ramified and expanded to such an extent, there needs must be capacious houses engaged in its conduct. One of the most prominent houses employed in the business is the reliable, well-known and justly popular house of G. J. Peacock. This concern was started in 1877 by the present proprietor, with about $2,500 capital, while now he requires as many thousand dollars as he had hundreds to conduct his business. He gives employment to eighteen males and fifty females regularly, and sometimes as many more, while he does an annual business of $60,000, extending throughout the Gulf States and in other parts of the United States. His sewing machines are operated by a gas engine, which is a great saving of strength to the operator. We place his name here, thus confident that his staunch character, energy and capital has advanced his pursuit to a first class position, and thereby entitles him to honorable mention. Peacock's name has become a synonym for fair dealing and elegant work, and his trade includes the most fashionable and "tony" of the men of this and adjoining cities. Nor have we a more liberal, conscientious and accommodating tradesman in our city, and if our own personal wishes could be gratified, we could seek no higher purpose in this regard than to see Peacock the absolute controller of ten times the trade he has, for this state of facts would undoubtedly contribute to a happier and better condition of the community in which he and his business are located.

RANKIN HOUSE BARBER SHOP—W. A. MAHONE, PROPRIETOR.

A first-class barber shop must always, in every community, hold a unique position, and the best proof of the esteem in which it is held is evinced by the amount of patronage which it enjoys. In Columbus one of the oldest and most popular establishment of this character is that of W. A. Mahone. His shop is 30x50 feet in dimension, affording ample room for a number of barbers, bathrooms, etc. Nothing is more refreshing than a good bath, and none are better prepared to accommodate you than the Rankin House Barber Shop. Clean towels, polite barbers, and prompt attention is the order of the day. They are well prepared to satisfy the most fastidious in hair-cutting, shaving or shampooing, being posted right up on all the latest styles of hair-cutting, etc. W. A. Mahone is a man well-known in Columbus, always sober and attentive to business; has had a number of years experience in his business, and always gives universal satisfaction. The shaving class of this city know W. A. Mahone to be *The* barber of Columbus.

J. KYLE & CO.—IMPORTERS AND JOBBERS OF DRY GOODS AND NOTIONS, AND MANUFACTURERS OF IRONCLAD BRAND PANTS AND OVERSHIRTS, NOS. 1106 AND 1108 BROAD STREET.

The growth of a city is always an interesting study, especially when viewed from some particular standpoint, and with reference to some particular department of human interest. Considering the rise of any populous center from its begin-

ning, we find a multitude of causes contributing to swell the volume of its prosperity, until the tide of its commercial and industrial progress resembles the flow of a mighty river, gathering into its channel the waters of an empire. But whatever influences may affect the aggregation of men into communities, there are certain natural conditions that must exist in order to give substantial and permanent character to such growth, and without which, increase is almost purely speculative, and prosperity temporary and delusive. Given these conditions, however, and they may be wasted by lack of intelligence to see the opportunity they offer, or of enterprise to make the most of it, while other points, with fewer natural advantages, but cultivating those with more energy, overcome the obstacles to their progress, and outstrip the sluggard in the race for wealth and power. Happily, the pioneers of Columbus were not lacking in either keenness of vision to descry the favorable features of the situation, nor in energy and ability to make use of them as the foundations of a thrifty and thriving community. Columbus is most favorably situated as to the great arteries and highways of commerce, having invaluable connections, by river and rail, her mercantile ramifications extending in every direction, and yearly growing larger and more important. One of the great factors in her progress and improvement has been her dry goods interest, and the history of her large wholesale jobbing houses, while a necessary and integral part of her statistical biography, is also interesting and valuable as an historical record, and useful for purposes of reference.

Mr. Joseph Kyle is one of our pioneer merchants in the dry goods line, commencing first in the retail business in 1838, under the firm name of Kyle & Barnett, and only eleven years after Columbus had received her charter of incorporation. In 1843 the firm name became J. & J. Kyle, and three years after they moved into a new store, built by them, No. 1116 Broad street. After ten years still larger quarters were required for the volume of business controlled by the firm and they moved to the building now occupied by Blanchard & Booth, and now owned by Mr. Kyle. Here the firm name was changed to its present style, and for more than a quarter of a century this was the leading retail dry goods house in this section. Recognizing the fact that dealers in the greater part of the adjoining States looked to Columbus, with her facilities for shipping, both by rail and water, for supplies in this line of trade, Messrs. J. Kyle & Co. decided to engage in an exclusively wholesale business, and moved into their present commodious building, which has three times been enlarged, but with abundant capital and a large, flourishing trade they are able to meet any demands made upon them. The facilities, so far as regard the premises occupied, are all that could be desired, 24,000 square feet of space being fully occupied, with a well-selected and comprehensive stock of dry goods suited to the trade in this section, including foreign and domestic manufactures and a full line of notions. They carry an average stock of $100,000, and their annual transactions reach $500,000. As manufacturers of the Ironclad Brand of pants and overshirts, this house has attained a wide-spread reputation, and supplies a large and increasing trade, a larger force of employees being required each year. An eight horse-power gas engine is provided for running the machines and a large number of operatives are constantly employed in the manufacturing department. The immense business of this house is thoroughly organized under different departments, managed by competent men, all under the constant supervision of the proprietors, and in these departments can probably be found more goods suited to the wants of the merchants in this section of country than can be found under any one roof in the city. The number of employees has lately been increased to ninety, of which thirty are males, sixty females, including a number of popular and efficient traveling salesmen, the monthly pay roll amounting to $2,300. Last year their sales reached $500,000, and their trade this year is much larger. Increasing capital and superior advantages have but prompted them to greater efforts in their lines than have been marked out. Such an enormous business gives them a great advantage over their competitors, enabling them to sell goods at close margins, and secure for themselves satisfactory profits. The commercial grasp of this house extends throughout Georgia, Alabama and Mississippi, and other States. Through all the years that this house has been in existence, all the changes it has undergone in the *personnel* of its proprietors, the trade incident to its long career and the depression in business at times, it has maintained, with brightening reputation, the perfect system, the high degree of mercantile integrity, the elevated business enterprise with which it was inaugurated by its founder, Mr. Joseph Kyle. Wealth is one of the elements of success, but it is non-effective and a resultless ingredient when not combined with business sagacity, which acts as a balance valve in the regulation of the supply of motive power which capital furnishes. In the narration of the progress and development of this great house, an illustration can be found of the grandly superior power of ability and clear thought, even in prosperity, and the subordination of capital to enterprise and adaptability. The senior member of this firm is of Scotch-Irish descent, and, although advanced in years, is brisk and alert, and bids fair to remain at the head of his colossal enterprise a number of years to come. He divides his time between his dry goods business and his plantation, called "The Bend," seven miles from the city, Mr. Kyle and his spirited bays being a well-known sight to our residents. Modest and retiring, he has never sought public office, but his voice has certain weight in public matters. His staff of assistants hold for him feelings of strong attachment and veneration, and his career is a valuable study to younger men in the business.

Mr. Frederick B. Gordon, the junior member of the firm, has been closely identified with the commercial interests of Columbus, having been formerly secretary of the Chattahoochee Valley Exposition Company, and president of the Columbus Board of Trade. He has assumed the active management of this enterprise, purchases all the goods for the dry goods and manufacturing departments, dictates all correspondence and decides all questions of credit. Under his management the business has received a new impetus, his genial and affable manners and cordial greeting of customers making himself many friends and adding patrons to their already extensive list.

Messrs. J. Kyle & Co. have the leading representative house in Columbus, and her interests and their name have become co-extensive with the South as a house of immense capital, superior stock and admirable business qualifications and judgment, with indomitable pluck, enterprise and energy, coupled with invariable courtesy and liberality.

SOUTHERN PLOW CO.—MANUFACTURERS OF PLOW STOCKS, STEEL, WROUGHT AND CAST IRON PLOW HOES, CAST PLOWS AND COTTON PLANTERS.

The prosperity of a manufactory is an indication both of superiority in the output and of the management. The Southern Plow Company was incorporated in 1877. The officers are: W. R. Brown, President, and G. W. Brown, Secretary and Treasurer, under whose capable management the business is guided in a course of true business principles and is enjoying a prosperous career, and it is an institution that would do honor to any city. Fifty hands are employed in the various departments, turning out material to the amount of from $100,000 to $125,000 per annum The product consists of plow stocks, plow hoes, steel, wrought and cast iron plow blades, points, plates, lap rings, grass rods, wings, castings, mold boards, single trees, heel bolts, clevis irons, cast plows, fixtures, etc.; in fact, the Company is fully equipped for furnishing every attachment connected with improved implements. Mr. G. W. Brown, the Secretary and Treasurer, has the business in charge, and keeps the popular demand up to a high standard, making shipments throughout the Southern States, regardless of sharp competition from other portions of the United States. Besides plows, this institution is manufacturing various kinds of cotton planters. The buildings occupy a space 300x100 feet, and we would state that the Southern Plow Company is valuable to Columbus in showing to the outside world that we have an industrious city.

COLUMBUS IRON WORKS—MANUFACTURES OF "COLUMBUS IRON WORKS ABSORPTION ICE MACHINE," STEAM ENGINES, BOILERS, TANKS, SAW MILLS, CANE MILLS, MILL AND GIN GEARING, COTTON PRESSES, CALENDER ROLLS, ETC., ETC., EEC.

Columbus has been brought conspicuously to the front as a manufacturing city by having within her limits the most extensive Iron Works in the entire South this side of Richmond, Va., and with this exception, there is not a wide difference, by any means—and in the class of work turned out there is no institution in the country in advance of the Columbus Iron Works. To one unacquainted with the magnitude of this plant it would be necessary to make a personal inspection to grasp the situation, as there are six acres covered with buildings, machinery and material, besides the towering stacks of lumber to be seen outside of the yards on the river banks. The hum of flying machinery, the clank of the mechanic's hammer, the puff of various steam engines here and there, the rumbling of planers, the hustle and bustle of 175 active mechanics, gives the appearance of a human bee-hive. Here is produced and finished "The Columbus Iron Works Improved Absorption Ice Machine," the most popular Ice machine made; there are also manufactured steam engines, boilers, tanks, saw mills, calender rolls, cotton presses, shafting, pulleys and hangers, hollow-ware, mill and gin gearing, cane mills, and sash, doors and blinds, the latter department is quite extensive. They also handle largely, rough and dressed lumber, shingles, laths and lime. The department for repairing work is also a feature, in this establishment, and quite a novelty in mechanics is to be seen here, which is in the welding of pipe coils together by electricity, in this line they are perpared to furnish the electric welded pipe coils of any description, and are executing an extensive amount of work. Pumps and Clayton's double Turbine water wheels are other products of this plant. The foundry is deserving of special mention, having every facility for turning out all kinds of work regardless of size and complication of patterns. About $80,000 per annum is paid out for labor. The business extends throughout the Southern States, and into Kansas, Illinois, Ohio, Indian Territory and Pennsylvania. Mr. Brown, the President, was reared in Columbus. He established these works in 1853, and in 1856 the same was incorporated. The officers now are, W. R. Brown, President; W. H. Brannon, Secretary and Treasurer, and W. Cook, Superintendent. Under this management the already large business, which, last year was about a half million dollars, is enjoying a healthful growth, and the establishment a pride to the State as well as the city.

SHEPHERD'S BRICK YARDS—SHEPHERD BROTHERS, PROPRIETORS.

To the collector of statistical data of the business interests of so great and progressive a city as Columbus, facts bearing on her most important facilities and resources, are more apparent than to the casual visitor, or even to a citizen. Special branches of industry, which are contributing more than most others, not only to her extension and improvement, but to her solidity and attractive appearance. Among these, all branches connected with the building facilities and resources, are worthy of special mention, and as Columbus is to-day furnishing most desirable material for manufacturing brick, and daily turning out large kilns of this product in superior grade, this class of industry deserves particular notice. We are led into these remarks by a visit to the works of Shepherd Brothers, at Shepherd's Brick Yards, and an inspection of their products, which are conceded to be the finest in quality, appearance, color, shape and smoothness, so far made. They manufacture brick from the Nolan-Madden machine, one of the very best brick machines, with every late improvement, and having the finest raw material to be found in the South, they are possessed of every facility for making the best brick to be found, and it is this grade that has brought Columbus to the front as a superior brick market. A forty-horse power engine and boiler is used to drive the machinery. Messrs. Shepherd Brothers own 200 acres of ground at their yards, which gives them an inexhaustible supply of the finest material. Their capacity is 9,000,000 brick yearly, including pressed, common and ornamental brick. The individual members of the firm are A. H. Shepherd and A. W. Shepherd. They were raised in Columbus, and are among our most influential and prominent citizens. This business begun in 1890, and since its inception has enjoyed a large and lucrative trade, which reaches throughout this State, Alabama and Florida. Continued on the plan of an honorable, straightforward policy, with which they have inaugurated their business, Shepherd Brothers will soon change into steady, vigorous maturity, and, their establishment become a representative one in its line.

THE STEAM PLANT & PLUMBING COMPANY—SANITARY PLUMBERS, No. 1145 FIRST AVENUE, G. B. HIETT, PROPRIETOR.

A good and reliable plumber is an indispensible necessity in every community, and in Columbus Mr. G. B. Hiett ranks with the best in all respects. Started in 1890 he has, by the excellence of his work, and the promptness with which it is performed, already attained the leading rank. His salesroom and workshop are large and commodious, a number of skillful hands are employed and the trade extends all over the city and country, and is annually increasing. Mr. Hiett does all manner of plumbing, gas and steam fitting, and hot air furnace works, these branches being their specialty. He also puts up pumps, bath tubs, etc., in the most thorough and workman-like manner, and every piece of work from their establishment is guaranteed. Mr. Hiett has been in the business since 1872, and is thoroughly familiar with all the branches of his business. He is a native of Tennessee, but has resided in Columbus for the past four years. The past honorable career of this house is an evidence of their fair and able business transactions, which has given universal satisfaction. Our readers will find this house one of the most reliable ones in this line of business in the State, and will reap a benefit in opening business relations with them. All work entrusted to them is sure of prompt attention and of being satisfactorily performed.

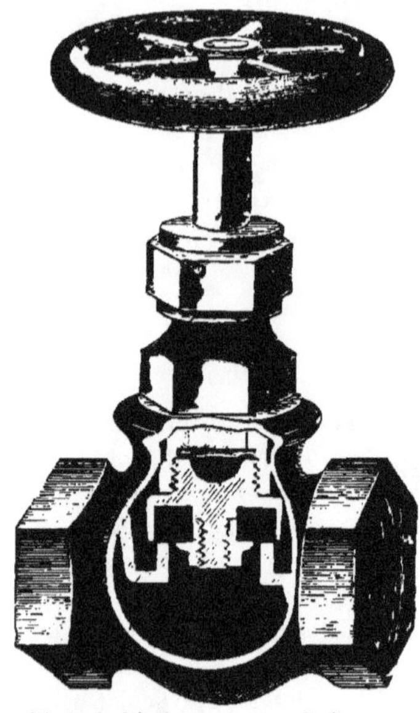

M. JOSEPH—JOBBER OF DRY GOODS, NOTIONS, ETC., 1131, 1133, 1135 AND 1137 BROAD STREET.

The business prosperity, enterprise and solidity of a city are, in a large measure, indicated by the extent and character of her business houses. Among them, the names of the wealthy old dry goods houses have become as familiar as household words. Their reputation extends that of their cities, and in no other branch do we find firms whose business transactions cover an extent of territory, limited only by the natural boundaries of the country. Columbus is favorably situated as to facilities for the transportation and distribution of merchandise. By rail she reaches the cities and towns of Georgia, Alabama and Florida. She controls the inland routes by river from here to the Gulf of Mexico, through a rich and fertile country

One of the great factors in her progress and improvement has been her dry goods interests, and the history of her large wholesale jobbing houses, while a necessary and an integral part of her biography, will be also interesting and valuable as an historical record, and useful for future reference. The mercantile history of M. Joseph is exceptionally interesting. Mr. Joseph begun retailing dry goods in Columbus in 1852, with a capital of eighty-five dollars, and to-day, is doing a business of seven hundred thousand dollars per annum, requiring the services of twenty efficient men to conduct the different departments. The average amount of stock corried is $125,000, and is complete in every particular. The stand of M. Joseph is at 1131, 1133, 1135 and 1137 Broad street, being centrally located and possessed of every convenience adapted to shipping and receiving goods.

About seventeen years ago the leading merchants began making efforts to secure reduced freight rates from the large markets to Columbus. Success was their reward, we were put upon an equal footing with the other principal points of this section, as regards freight rates. Mr. Joseph (then in the retail business) realizing the situation, changed his system from the retail to the wholesale trade, and soon had his salesmen traveling the rich territory adjacent to this city, and through his pluck, enterprise and energy, has reached out further and further for business, and, year after year a large increase has resulted, until now this house has taken rank with the leading wholesale establishments in this part of the South. dry goods and notions are rolled out of the establishment of M. Joseph every day destined to Mineral regions of Alabama, the Lumber districts of Georgia throughout the Land of Flowers and fruits, up and down the fertile valley of the Chattahoochee, and on the Gulf coast, and into the cities, towns and villages of all this section embraced in the three States. This leading representative merchant of Columbus, M. Joseph, is widely known, his name has become familiar throughout the South, his reputation that of a progressive and thorough business manager.

KELLY & CO.—Wholesale Grocers, Nos. 10 to 16 Tenth Street.

The term grocer was formerly used to signify a merchant who sold the staple coffee, tea, etc., in gross, but with the progress in trade, the business of the grocer became more comprehensive and his stock enlarged, including many articles carried by houses or branches as specialties. Mercantile establishments are divided into two classes: those who deal in necessities or staples, and those who deal in luxuries and specialties; the latter are useful, but their patronage is confined to the wealthy and fashionable; the first are indispensible—their custom comes from all classes, their wares supply wants of actual necessity to the health, comfort and vigor of man. In this class are included grocers whose main stock consists of articles entering into the food supply, in some instances articles of luxury are included, as liquors, canned goods, tobaccos, etc. There is no more important factor in the commercial and industrial growth of a city than the grocery trade, and no more unerring criterion by which to estimate its enterprise. Flourishing, well conducted and prosperous grocery firms indicate the existence of energy and industry, which are the surest evidences of progress and the development of commercial interests. The wholesale grocery trade will always occupy a foremost position in Columbus, as it conduces, in a very great degree, to her importance as a mercantile point. This city has several houses, the trade of which will compare most favorably with those of the large Eastern and Western cities, and among these houses there are none better entitled to special mention than the establishment of Kelly & Co. This concern was started by Farmer, Kelly & Co. in 1888, the present firm succeeding to the business in 1890. The extensive premises of the establishment are conveniently located on Tenth street, with a building 100 feet square, two stories in height, which is fully utilized in the prosecution of business. The stock carried is always full and complete in all departments, and is commensurate with the business, the value being placed at $30,000. An inspection of the business premises evidences the perfect system of the establishment, various departments moving with regularity, all under the management of the proprietors. In the stock will be found every conceivable article pertaining to the trade. Ten employees are required in selling and handling goods and the trade extends throughout Alabama, Florida and Georgia, the annual transactions reaching half a million dollars. The individual members of the firm are Messrs. M. W. Kelly and John R. Kelly. They were born in Central Georgia, but moved to Southwestern Alabama when boys, and gained their excellent business experience there. Mr. M. W. Kelly was engaged in business in Columbia, Ala., until 1888, when he came to Columbus. Mr. John R. Kelly was in business in Newton, Ala., until the present house was formed, when he became a member. These are the qualifications, resources and facilities of a representative firm of our city's commercial history of this period, a practical illustration that enterprise, sound business principles and commendable ambition will assure success, wheresoever the location may be, and that they, not chance, are the prime elements in progress.

MRS. A. POSADA—Dealer in Cigars, Tobacco, Pipes, Etc., No. 16, Twelfth Street.

In a careful review of the various commercial industries of Columbus, it is plainly observable that a detailed mention of each evidences great advantages which some possess over others in the same line of business. The result of longer experience and a greater, natural aptitude to their particular trade or profession. In the cigar and tobacco business, Mrs. A. Posada may be said to have attained her reputation and prosperous trade from both of the essentials above mentioned, being one of the pioneers in the business in this section, with an experience of thirty-three years, and a practical knowledge of the business in all of its details. She established herself in business in this city in 1876 with small capital, while the city was still in its youth, and before it had put on metropolitan habiliments. This business, conducted with energy, close application and industry, backed by her superior knowledge of its requirements, has been successful from the start, and Mrs. Posada has succeeded in building up a lucrative patronage. She carries a complete stock—consisting of imported and domestic cigars in all grades and qualities, the most popular brands of chewing and smoking tobaccos, pipes and smoker's sundries generally. Her premises are commodious and convenient, 50x100 feet in size. Her trade, besides being largely local, extends through this immediate section, reaches $5,000 annually. This house is justly entitled to the consideration and patronage of the public, and the proprietress to the esteem that energy, honesty and industry always inspire.

TOL. Y. CRAWFORD—ATTORNEY-AT-LAW, 1155½ BROAD STREET.

Among the young men who have, in a few years, written their names high on the tablet of fame, none in our city are more worthy of the success they have achieved than Tol. Y. Crawford, the promising young attorney-at-law, at present City Solicitor of Columbus. Mr. Crawford was born in Kentucky in 1860, and came to Columbus in 1883, studying law with Mr. Reese Crawford, and was admitted to the bar in 1885. He was a student at Center College, Louisville, Ky. It was necessary for him to remain with the people of Columbus but a short time ere they discovered his superior ability, as is evidenced by his election as city attorney in 1889, and again in 1890. He is a pushing young man, who is bound to win success in his chosen profession, and in the end hold a leading place in the law.

CENTRAL LINE OF BOATS.

On the 29th day of November, 1828, a pole boat named the Rob Roy, with a cargo of merchandise consigned to J. Fontaine, Maherry, Love & Co., landed at Columbus—this being the first craft to touch at this point in the history of the town. The Rob Roy was from Apalachicola, Fla., and was propelled with long poles, operated by the roustabouts. The first steamboat, the Virginia, landed here May 25th, 1829, from Apalachicola, and on the 28th of December, made her second trip here and returned ladened with 400 bales of cotton for New Orleans. The first steamer owned by citizens of Columbus was the "Georgian," built at Pittsburg, Pa., and made the trip from Pittsburg to Columbus in fifteen days. And with the progress of time and growth of the country, the river traffic kept pace, and at the present day the amount of business transacted on the Chattahoochee river, between Columbus and Apalachicola, is of marked importance, and of the several lines of steamboats in this trade, that of the Central Line of Boats deserves special mention. Mr. Samuel J. Whitesides is the proprietor of the line, and having the experience of thirty years in the business, and being a successful and enterprising man, he is in a position to know the requirements of his numerous patrons, and by his upright transactions has grown in popularity to an enviable degree. There are two large packets in the trade, requiring the employment of thirty-seven hands, drawing a pay-roll of $1200 per month. These steamers ply the Chattahoochee, Apalachicola, Flint and Chipola rivers, doing a large and extensive business. Mr. George B. Whitesides is a son of the proprietor, and for a number of years has held the position of manager, which position he holds with ability, and having been reared in the business is, as a natural consequence, quite familiar with every detail in connection, and for this reason is the Central Line of Boats so popular and doing such a thriving business.

RIDDLE & NUCKOLLS—Wholesale Tobacco and Cigars, Corner Fourteenth Street and First Avenue.

In endeavoring to preserve some record of our commercial firms by historical notes, our object in introducing this department of our work is attributed more to a desire to gather together remembrances of such interesting nature, rather than to seek opportunity for personal compliment. But it is quite admissible for us to say that the house of Riddle & Nuckolls, wholesale tobacconists, belongs to that class of enterprising business firms which have given the city her reputation abroad. This enterprise was started in 1887 by Mr. J. W. Riddle, and in 1889 Mr. J. K. Nuckolls was admitted to the firm. The business premises consist of half an acre of ground covered with buildings, including their large store room for tobacco and cigars. Messers. Riddle & Nuckolls are agents for the Humming Bird, Fat Possum, Lucy Neal and Eli Tobaccos, and Big Nickel navy Tobacco, "*Little Carrie*," Spanish Flag and Custom House Cubanna cigars, and Bower's Three Thistle Snuff. A large and flourishing trade is transacted throughout Georgia, Florida and Alabama. Nine employees are required in the business, and all orders are filled with promptness and satisfaction to all concerned. The stock carried is valued at $15,000, and the transactions reach $100,000. All of the business operations of this concern are under the direct supervision of the proprietors, enabling them to guarantee the purity and good quality of all goods they put upon the market, and has given their goods a reputation second to none. The greatest care and attention is bestowed in every department, making their house one of the *most prominent* of our flourshing business houses. Mr. J. W. Riddle has lived in Columbus thirty-four years, and may be appropriately classed among our most prosperous and enterprising merchants. He has had fifteen years experience in this line of trade, and thoroughly understands its requirements. Mr. Nuckolls is also a native Georgian, and is widely known for his sterling business qualities. He was connected for a number of years with the firm of J. Kyle & Co., of this city, also proprietor of the large wholesale hat house of J. K. Nuckolls & Co., Chattanooga, Tenn. No firm enjoys a higher position commercially, which considering the liberal and enterprising spirit that actuates its operations, is as natural as it is justly deserved.

VERNON HOTEL BARBER SHOP—J. A. Neals, Proprietor.

When you want an easy shave,
As good as barber ever gave;
Call on me at my saloon—
Morning, evening or at noon!
I cut and dress the hair with grace,
To suit the custom of the face;
My rooms are neat, towels clean,
Shears sharp and razors keen:
Everything I think you'll find,
To suit the face and please the mind.
All my art and skill can do,
If you will call I will do for you.

BLANDFORD & GRIMES—Attorneys-at-Law.

In our column, while reviewing the trade and conditions of trade of our city, we do not wish to pass by that class of men who is so potent in advancing the interests of every community—the lawyer. The Bar of Muscogee county might well be termed a galaxy of stars, but there are none more talented or deserving of more notice than our friends, Judge Blandford and Captain Grimes. Mr. Blandford, the senior member of the firm, is a brilliant man, of unusual learning, fully rounded out in all the departments of his profession. Possessed of judicial mind and force of character, he was placed on the Supreme Bench in 1883, which place he filled with honor alike to himself and the State until 1891. He is a native of Warren county and came to Columbus in 1869. He studied law with Judge R. V. Howderman, in Jones county, and was admitted to the Bar in 1844 under a special act of the Legislature. His health was impaired while suffering the hardships of a campaign in Mexico in '46 and '48. He served through all the years of the late war. Pleasant, learned and interesting, he is a superior man who has hosts of friends, and deserves them. Mr. T. W. Grimes is a native of Greene county. He served through two years of the war, and shortly afterward entered political life. He had been a brave soldier in war and now, in politics, he was a rival worthy of the steel of a Knight. He was elected to the lower house of Congress in 1868, and in 1875 to the Senate of his State. From 1878 to 1880 he was Solicitor-General of the Chattahoochee Circuit. His people again called him to represent them in the Fifty-second Congress, and again in the stormy Reed Congress, he nobly defended the rights of the minority. Mr. Grimes has been a close student from boyhood, studying law with Rumsey & Lamar, he was early admitted to practice. He is an able lawyer, an honest citizen and a noble gentleman.

M. T. BERGAN—Wholesale Liquors, Bottling Works, Manufacturer of Ice, and Agent Christian Moerlein Beer, Corner Broad and Dillingham Streets.

Worthy of liberal mention in any work relating to the general business activities of a city like Columbus, are all enterprises which conduce to the convenience and benefit of the general community, claiming importance as leading industries, which give reputation to a city for manufacturing enterprise and progressive spirit, whether by individual or corporate action. This city has reason to be proud of her manufacturing interests, and of no one concern more so than that of Mr. Bergan. This establishment was founded seven years ago by the present proprietor, who has done as much, perhaps, to extend the reputation of Columbus and bring the excellence of her products before the people of this section as any other firm in the city. A complete and well selected assortment of wholesale liquors is kept in stock, and in the bottling department a large business is transacted. As manufacturer of ice, Mr. Bergan fills a long felt want in this part of the South, and supplies a large trade. The business premises are 75x147 feet in size and contain apparatus and appliances of the most excellent character, the facilities being fully equal to the capacities of an immense trade. Twenty employees are required in the transaction of business and in the manufacturing department, and orders are filled in a prompt and careful manner. Mr. Bergan enjoys an extended and flourishing trade throughout Georgia, Florida and Alabama, and he is fully prepared to meet any demands made upon him for goods in his line. The ice factory turns out seven tons of ice per day, and Mr. Bergan has a branch house in Griffin, where he manufactures ice also, and supplies that point and country tributary to it. The career of Mr. Bergan has been most successful, on account of the ability and skill with which he has operated his establishment, and the liberal, enterprising policy that has characterized its business. Mr. Bergan was born in Ireland fifty-four years ago. He has resided in Columbus for thirty years, and is well known and popular among our people. He has always been esteemed a man of unusual energy, strong force of character and liberal business characteristics, his business enterprises always occupying a prominent position in the community, uniformly managing his business with skill and success. He deserves the praise and congratulations of the citizens for building up this splendid system of economy and thrift in their midst, and we would here take occasion to remark that such men build up the reputation and trade of cities and enable them to retain it.

SINGER MANUFACTURING COMPANY—12 Twelfth Street.

The hum of the sewing machine is heard all over the land. There is no voice in which there is more music than in its delicate click, for it means a cessation for weary women, a folding of tired hands, and a closing of weary eyes which before the sewing machine came to make the tiresome seams, must have worked long after the rest of the household had sought their couch. There are few houses in the land in which the name of the "Singer Machine" is not familiar. It is not excelled by any sewing machine in the market, both as to simplicity of machinery and beauty of woodwork. Its management is so easy that a little child may soon learn to work it, and its "light running" is so famous that the most delicate ladies are enabled to use it without detriment to health. The attachments are unsurpassed, and a woman can make almost anything that fancy may suggest. The ware-rooms and office for Columbus and surrounding counties is located at No. 12 Twelfth street, being tastefully and handsomely fitted and furnished, with sufficient room to accommodate many hundred machines. The manager of the Columbus branch is C. C. Gunter, who gives all his time and attention to this work; he has accomplished much for the machine in the territory under his supervision and control. Energy and business tact superior to that shown by this gentleman is rarely evinced, and the company thoroughly appreciate his success. The high standing he enjoys is justly due him, being a man of sterling worth and keen intelligence. Everybody contemplating purchasing a new machine should not fail to examine "The Singer" before they purchase, as it gives entire satisfaction in every case. It presents a beautiful appearance, is light running, speedy, silent and easy. "To try it is to buy it."

RHODES BROWNE—General Fire Insurance Agent, Office 1048 Broad Street, Georgia Home Building.

The principle of insurance is founded upon the doctrine of probabilities. According to this doctrine, if we take a sufficiently extended range of instances, the probability of a certain event happening can be ascertained with a considerable degree of accuracy. It is in this way that insurers calculate their risks and estimate their premiums. From extended series of observations and carefully prepared tables they know the chances of the event insured against happening, and determine the amount of the premium accordingly. The business of insurance is generally carried on by companies having a large subscribed capital, by means of which they are able without difficulty to meet any heavy loss, while their premiums being proportioned to their risks, their profit is, at an average, independent of such contingencies. The advantages of insurance are very great. While to a merchant the loss of his building and stock might be a very serious matter, he can thus, by the payment of a certain sum, provide against it, so that he may carry on his business with a feeling of perfect security. The insurer is usually called an underwriter, because he writes his name at the foot of the policy. Columbus has a number of agencies representing foreign and domestic companies, among the most prominent of which is that of Mr. Rhodes Browne. This agency was originally established in 1859, and represents some of the best and most reliable companies of the world. A glance at the companies represented by Mr. Browne will carry the convincing proof of their worth and ability: Georgia Home Insurance Company, of Columbus, Ga., Queen Insurance Company, of Liverpool, England, Commercial Union Assurance Company, of London, England, Norwich Union Insurance Society, of Norwich, England, Greenwich Insurance Company, of New York, and Central City Insurance Company, of Selma, Alabama, with combined assets reaching $10,000,000.

J. W. ENNIS—General Merchandise.

One of the largest and most prominent retail establishments in the city devoted to the general merchandise business, is that of J. W. Ennis, situated on Rose Hill. The building occupied is 35x80 feet, and admirably arranged throughout for the handling of his extensive business. He carries a complete stock of all kinds of goods, amounting to from $2,000 to $5,000, according to the demands of the season, and does an annual business of $18,000 in the city and surrounding country. The merchant who heads this article is one of that class, who, through business astuteness, working with small capital, but having that business sagacity and foresight, has placed himself on a footing by the side of those whose capital at the start was much greater. Mr. Ennis is thoroughly posted in his business, has been brought up in it. He is fully alive to the wants of the public, and has the honor and esteem of all who have business relations with him. He is a live, progressive and enterprising citizen, always has the interest of Columbus at heart, ready and willing to do anything to advance the city's interest.

THE SOUTHERN COLLEGE OF MUSIC—Incorporated Aug. 24, 1889.

In the April of 1886 Mme. Antoinette Bronsil-Grant and Prof. H. McCormack opened a school of music in Columbus, and so thorough and satisfactory was the instruction given that it immediately met with flattering success. After three years of ever increasing prosperity, this school was re-organized into the Southern College of Music, which was duly chartered by the courts August 24, 1889. The object of this change was to enlarge the field of labor, and to plan and follow a more complete course of study than was possible in the smaller school. In order that the work done by this school may compare favorably with that of any other similar school, only the very finest teachers and musicians have been employed. The faculty for the present year consists of: Mme. A. B. Grant, Piano, Organ and Singing; H. McCormack, Piano, Flute and Theory; Alexander de Czeke, Violin and Theory; Carl Hessler, Piano, Violin, Cornet and Orchestra Playing. The preparation of teachers is a specialty, and the fortunate holder of a diploma from the Southern College of Music will have a choice of many lucrative positions. For catalogue containing full particulars of course of study, methods employed, etc., address A. G. Grant, Secretary and Treasurer, 1221 Fourth avenue, Columbus, Ga.

COLUMBUS WATER WORKS CO.

Since water, like climate, has a sanitary bearing on a city's advantages, it is of the highest importance to have a bountiful supply of that good and wholesome beverage, so freely bestowed by God himself to "nourish and invigorate His creatures and to beautify His footstool." Then, too, villages and hamlets, and even towns and cities, are oftener than from any other cause located in proximity to good water. For all manufacturing purposes, for laundry requirements and for culinary needs, as well as for the extinguishment of fires, Columbus has a water supply that is second to none in the entire State. For many years Columbus jogged along in the old way without any system of water works; true, for drinking purposes, nearly every house had its well or cistern, but there was no water for fire protection, and when the city was visited by this fiend the old "Bucket Brigade" was called forth to extinguish the flames. Soon, enterprising men and capital came, and a contract was made by Thos. R. White with the city, and the water works were established. The plant consists of a number of miles of pipe, varying from 6 to 12 inches in diameter; a stand-pipe and two reservoirs—the reservoirs being located in Lee County, Ala., about three miles from the city, and capable of storing about one hundred and forty-five millions of gallons of water. These reservoirs are fed by never failing springs and are at an elevation of 119 feet above the level on which the city stands, and therefore the water is delivered entirely by gravity, affording an average pressure of 40 pounds for fire protection, sanitary purposes and general use by consumers, and no pumping is necessary to produce this pressure. The stand-pipe is 20 feet in diameter and 120 feet high; capacity 350,000 gallons. The Company has a contract with the city and receives in hydrant rentals, together with water rents from consumers, about thirty thousand dollars per annum. The expenses of operating the plant are about six thousand dollars per annum, which is a very gratifying showing for the short time it has been operated by the present management. The plant is gradually increasing, it being in contemplation soon to erect another reservoir with a storage capacity of four hundred millions of gallons which, added to the present one hundred and forty-five millions, would give a grand total of five hundred and forty-five millions storage capacity, thereby looking far into the future needs of Columbus.

Mr. H. H. Epping is President (and also President of the Chattahoochee National Bank), Mr. J. G. Beasley is Secretary and Treasurer, and Mr. M. H. Tuggle is Superintendent. These are men fully conversant with the business in which they are engaged, with broad and liberal views and great expectations for the future of Columbus. They are men of the highest social standing, and enjoy the esteem of their fellow citizens in the highest degree, and to them much credit is due for the success their works have achieved.

PIEDMONT CIDER WORKS—Corner Fourteenth Street and First Avenue.

A man who creates a new and profitable branch of manufacture is a public benefactor, but he who, in addition to this furnishes the people with an article of drink which partakes of nearly all the nutritive qualities of a beverage without the frequent diletarious effects of violent stimulants—an article which is healthgiving in all its properties, and the general use of which cannot fail to elevate the health average of the people. A man who does this, absolutely deserves the gratitude of his fellow man. We desire, therefore, to cite an instance in point: Prior to 1890 there was not a cider manufactory for bottling cider in Columbus, but in that year a factory was started by Riddle & Nuckolls, who built up such an enormous trade that it was necessary to take another partner.

in 1892 Mr. Ed. Shepherd was taken in, thus making the firm consist of J. W. Riddle, J. K. Nuckolls and E. A. Shepherd. The Piedmont Cider Company and Soda Works have a daily bottling capacity of 250 bottles of soda water, and 100 kegs cider and seventy-five dozen champagne cider, and a specialty is made of bottling all kinds of cider, soda and mineral waters. A glance at their price list shows that among their productions in keg, half-barrel and barrel, are refined fruit grape, peach, orange and cherry, sand refined grape and peach, plain peach and strawberry, pure apple and crabapple, ginger ale and ambrosia ciders, all of which they make the highest grade, and are prepared to furnish in any quantities. They use none but the most improved machinery, a combination of the best English and American manufactures. Their factory covers one-quarter acre of ground, giving employment to eleven hands, who receive good wages for their labor. Their's is one of the largest of its kind in the South, and is under the management of Mr. E. A. Shepherd, who is a native Georgian, with ten years experience in the business, and is recognized for his excellent business qualities, high integrity, and is a live, progressive citizen. Such men are the backbone of a city's prosperity. They never hold back, but move on with the car of progress.

TURNER BROS.—MANUFACTURING PHARMACISTS, 1002 BROAD STREET, UNDER RANKIN HOUSE.

The importation, manufacture and dispensing of drugs and chemicals is one of the most important branches of business in this country, as well as the most responsible and worthy of attention. In old times the medical practitioner compounded his own preparations, kept his supply of drugs and dispensed them. The legitimate druggist is of comparatively modern origin, as a distinct profession, in this country. We were until about 1815 dependent on foreign talent and skill, most of the prominent articles and pharmaceutical preparations being imports from German, English and French laboratories. But of late years, the educated druggist having entered the field, the apothecary has been separated from the mere shop-keeper, and the business elevated to a professional rank. Much attention, too, of recent years has been directed to the complete professional education of pharmacists, and colleges for that purpose have been established in the metropolitan cities of the country, a diploma being now considered a *sine quo non* for the successful and reliable pharmacist. The drug business covers a large field, embracing a great variety of distinct articles, and the requisite knowledge of each and its properties and effects, which every competent druggist should have, makes it a profession requiring unremitting study and profound research. The character of an establishment, like that of individuals, is generally measured by its success, and, if professional, by its merit. In presenting a record of the commercial industries of Columbus, it is important to select representative establishments, and to consider those most successful and worthy of confidence. One of the largest, most complete and attractive drug establishments in the city is that of Turner Bros., located at No. 1002 Broad street, under the Rankin House. These gentlemen started in business together in 1889 with limited capital, and have attained a fair share of trade in their line from our citizens. They carry a most complete and well selected assortment of articles usually found in houses of this description, and also are sole proprietors and manufacturers of Turner's Liver Pills, Picine and Diarrhœa Cordial. Their stock is valued at $9,000, and the annual transactions, which are local in character, will reach $25,000. Three courteous, attentive and capable assistants are employed, the monthly disbursements reaching $225. Messrs. J. P. and J. C. Turner are the individual members of the firm, Mr. J. C. Turner occupying a prominent position with Tarrant & Co., of New York. Mr. J. P. Turner was born in Columbus in December, 1859, and commenced the study of his profession in 1877. The success of Turner Bros. in competition with the old established houses is not only surprising, but the best indication of their superior merit and enterprising business policy.

N. B.—Messrs. Turner Bros. make a specialty of manufacturing fine soda water. Ask for their recipes.

F. B. TOMBLIN—Dealer in Staple and Fancy Groceries, Girard, Ala.

The grocery trade in all towns and cities has its representatives who, both on account of the superior class of goods they handle and the reputation of the house for straightforward dealings, are acknowledged to be the leaders. Such a position is occupied by Mr. F. B. Tomblin. He deals in all kinds of Staple and Fancy Groceries and does a large business annually. Mr. Tomblin makes a specialty of "Ballard's Obelisk Flour" and fine water-ground meal. Especial notice is due to his finely and well-selected stock of canned goods, candies, etc. He also carries a full line of notions. He takes a delight in keeping up with all the best goods that can be had, giving his customers entire satisfaction in every respect. Mr. Tomblin is a native Georgian, but has been in this city for three years, and is well acquainted with his trade. He is a gentleman of pleasant manners, and holds the respect and confidence of the community in which he lives. As a business man he bears an enviable reputation for promptness, business ability and integrity.

V. R. CANTRELL—Groceries, Dry Goods, Shoes, Etc., Hamilton Avenue and Robinson Street, Rose Hill.

To no branch of commerce can Columbus point with more pride than to her immense trade in groceries. Within her incorporate limits are establishments whose colossal proportions would do honor to much larger cities. As it is not our intention to make comparative statements in this article relative to the wholesale trade of the city, we will at once confine ourselves to the facilities provided for the supply of our every day wants. Perhaps the most popular grocer in this section of the city is Mr. V. R. Cantrell, whose well arranged establishment is located at junction of Hamilton avenue and Robinson street, telephone number 272. Mr. Cantrell commenced business at his present location in 1890, and has had a very satisfactory increase. By his sterling integrity, energy and perseverance, has built up his trade to its present desirable proportions. His store-room is capacious, finished in a neat and attractive manner, and his goods present a very inviting appearance. His stock consists of a full line of well selected groceries of all kinds; also staple dry goods, shoes, etc. He employs two assistants, who are ever ready with affable and kind manners to serve his customers. Citizens will find this establishment a most desirable one with which to form business relations. His goods are of the best brands, and sold at bottom prices. Mr. Cantrell is a native of Georgia, and was born in Paulding county 1845; has resided in Columbus for the past seventeen years. He is a reliable and trustworthy man, and has established his business on a solid basis, entitling him to a high position among the business men of the city.

H. F. JACKSON, M. D.--Phenix City, Ala.

No history of a city's trade and commerce and industries would be complete without making special mention of those persons engaged in the practice of the learned arts and professions. In Phenix City the various professional places are filled with men fitted by nature and education for them, and this is especially true of the gentleman whose name heads this article. Dr. Jackson is a native of Georgia, but has been practicing in Phenix City and surrounding country for the past five years. During this time he has made many warm friends. He makes a specialty of female diseases, and owing to his marked success in that line, with his courteous manner, has made him a general favorite with the ladies. In all the branches of his profession, his work is the best. We will say to those of our readers who are so unfortunate as to be sufferers, and especially of the female diseases, that no one can be employed who will handle their case with more skill, kindness and patience.

MRS. S. J. SAULS—Florist, 732 First Avenue.

To the lover of the beautiful in nature there is nothing more grateful than the presence of flowers—nothing that so powerfully appeals to our better and softer sympathies—nothing, in fact, more ennobling and refining than the love and taste for nature's own adornment and decoration, the lovely and fragrant rose and its kindred. The love of flowers is an unmistakable sign of refinement of a people, and where that love or fancy exists the rough side of human nature finds no abiding place. There can be no more delightful or interesting industry than that of a florist. Among those, however, that have secured, by their enterprise and energy, more than usual prominence in this department may be mentioned Mrs. S. J. Sauls, who possesses qualifications which place her in the first rank as a botanist and florist. Mrs. Sauls commenced this business in 1885, and with her native industry, energy and adoption to her pursuit soon largely increased. The conservatories, six in number, are tastefully and practically arranged with scientific accuracy, and heated with the best approved appliances for generating heat with hot water. Mrs. Sauls brings to her work all the devotion and care of a true love—treating her plants as a loving parent—finding in her pursuit personal pleasure. This establishment is spoken of as one of the largest of the kind in the State, and is to the visitors a shrine where they can see what devotion and untiring labor can develop, flowers and flowering shrubs so beautiful and varied that the eye fairly wearies with their myriad of colors. Here will be found a profuse display of exotic and native plants in endless variety to gratify the love of the beautiful—roses, the empress of flowers, the gentle geranium, verbenas, coleus, the graceful and lovely fuchsias, tuberoses, stately gladiolies, and matchless lilies, pansies, the cactus of the desert, the fern of the mountain glade, etc. Mrs. Sauls plans rustic rockeries, fancy aquariums, and designs any style of floral decorations with perfect taste and artistic skill. She is prepared to furnish bedding or pot plants or cuttings, as desired, from her well selected stock on short notice, and her bouquets, baskets, chaste and appropriate funeral emblems defy competition. Mr. Sauls, an esteemed gentleman of culture and taste, shares with pleasure in these endeavors of his wife, and attends to the wants of the patrons of the house with courtesy and kindness. He is thoroughly conversant with the details of this most delicate business, and is an experienced botanist, who has built up a high reputation in his line of business, and who can and will maintain it.

TORBERT & FLOYD—Millers' and Packers' Agents and Jobbers of Dressed Meats.

On June 1st, 1891, two young men established a new departure in the mercantile line here, and have grown to greatness in this line, which has done much towards bringing Columbus prominently to the front as a commercial centre. The gentlemen referred to are Messrs. E. A. Torbert and John A. Floyd, the individual members of the subject of this sketch. Their success, since the inauguration of the business, has been phenomenal, the transactions reaching to an annual business of $1,250,000, the largest of any house in the city. Their trade extends throughout Georgia, Florida and Alabama, their sales on mill products alone reaching $1,500 daily. The actual daily output of their mills being 200 barrels of flour and 500 bushels of meal, and of the very highest grade, and as it is well known that the quality of flour depends largely upon the miller's ability, we make note of the fact that two skilled millers, having twenty years experience, are employed, which accounts for the popularity of the brands of flour produced by them, the following being a list of these brands: "Royal Patent," "Peerless," "Legal Tender" and "Regulator." Messrs. Torbert & Floyd have displayed an unusual amount of enterprise in gathering the facilities for handling meats, and it may be interesting to note that they handle a greater variety of cuts than any house in the South Atlantic States, which is saying a great deal; but nevertheless it is a fact. Many of these cuts were novelties to this trade until this firm introduced them. Besides the clear, long and short ribbed sides, both in smoked and dry salted, they have the English square cut ribs, backs, bellies, American cut shoulders, English cut shoulders, and bacon and dry salt shoulders of both cuts, and various grades of sugar-cured breakfast bacon, hams, picnic hams, boneless hams, mutton, fresh pork, beef, veal and other products. The stock of meats usually carried varies from 100,000 to 200,000 pounds. This firm has supplied a long felt want in Columbus by erecting a cold storage for fresh meats, the capacity of which is four cars. A stock of choice Western beef, pork, mutton, veal, etc., is kept on hand, and dealt out to the retailer as he needs it. Their large salesrooms and warehouse is situated at the corner of Tenth street and Seventh avenue. Side-tracks connecting with every railroad centering here are built to their doors, which gives them excellent facilities for shipping and receiving. Grain is also handled extensively. Their sausage department is deserving of special notice, as they are manufacturing high grades, and in large lots. During the past twelve months their sales have reached 425,000 pounds. The superiority of the quality is evidenced from the fact that they are shipping this sausage as far as Selma, Ala., on the west to the Atlantic coast on the east, and from Tampa, Fla., on the south to Atlanta, Ga., on the north.

Mr. Torbert is just twenty-two years of age and Mr. Floyd twenty-five. This is a remarkable age at which to handle such an immense business, but it happens that their business training has been good, and that they are talented for this kind of work, and that they work early and late and do this work on a sound business policy. Such men go far toward building up a city, and we bespeak for them, as we do for Columbus, a solid and prosperous growth.

WILLIAMS & BOOKER—Dealers in Groceries and General Plantation Supplies, Phenix City, Ala.

There is, perhaps, no house in the city of Columbus more worthy of an extended notice in a work of this description, giving, as it does, a detailed review of the trade, commerce and industries of Columbus, than the one which heads this article. There is no other branch of the mercantile business in which there is so much capital employed actively as in the dry goods and grocery trade. We take great pleasure in writing the history of this house. It is quite admissible for us to say that Williams & Booker, dealers in all kinds of groceries and plantation supplies, at Phenix City, belongs to that class of staunch, sagacious merchants, who have been prominently identified with the commercial interest of their city for seven years, and to whose enterprise and perseverance, as well as sterling conduct and uprightness, those interests are indebted for much of their present vigor and development. Mr. Williams runs a large dry goods establishment next door to his grocery, under the style of Williams & Co., composed of Messrs. Warren Williams, John Summersgill and William McCollister, all good, influential business men. This house has a very extensive trade, reaching far out in the surrounding country. It is the leading store in Phenix City. They carry a varied and well selected stock of dry goods, clothing, boots, shoes, hats, etc., with prices that can't be beat by the wholesale houses. The premises consist of two separate stores, 24 x 60 feet each, in which is carried a large and comprehensive stock.

Mr. Williams is a native of Alabama, and has long been identified with the people of Phenix City. He is a gentleman of high business integrity and honesty, and, like his partner, enjoys the confidence of his fellow-citizens. Mr. Leslie Booker, one of the junior partners, is a young man deserving much credit. He started with this firm as a clerk about six years since, and, by close attention to business and honorable and fair dealings, has gained for himself an interest in the business, holding also the responsible position of book-keeper. In Mr. Thos. Coulter he has a clerk of rare business qualities, a strictly temperate, conscientious and moral young man. As a firm, they have all the elements of success, and we predict for them a continuance of their large and lucrative trade.

V. J. PEKOR—Watchmaker and Jeweler, 1034 Broad Street.

The jewelry trade, with its vast and exclusive American manufactories, has been the growth of the last half century. Except in the diamond and richer work in gold and precious stones, which were formerly confined to the wealthy, it may be said that American ingenuity made it possible for poor men to enjoy this great pleasure which the possession and display of jewelry has always caused among men. Mr. Pekor is now the leading man among the many jewelers of this city. He succeeded C. H. Lequin in 1889 with very limited capital, now carrying a stock of $20,000 in value, and doing a satisfactory business of about $30,000 per annum. Mr. Pekor is entitled to special mention for the admirable taste displayed in the selection of a very comprehensive stock of high class goods and rare articles pertaining to the trade. He carries the choicest line of diamonds and fine watches, which he makes a specialty, besides genuine French mariner and bronze clocks; also a complete assortment of American clocks, tableware, fruit stands, cake baskets, entree dishes, jewelry cases and goods suitable for bridal presents. In sterling silverware, such articles as knives and forks, spoons, ice cream sets, fish sets, and all the latest designs in fine plush and chamois cases. His stock of plateware cannot be surpassed; in fact, you will find everything in the line that is carried as complete an assortment as you will find in the large Eastern houses. Mr. Pekor is a native of Bohemia, Europe, but has been in this city for fourteen years. He is a thorough, trained jeweler having served a long apprenticeship in Europe, and it may be said that

he has been brought up in the business. He is a public-spirited citizen, an energetic and thorough reliable business man, possessing the entire confidence and respect of the community in which he resides. He is an example of marked success which industry, skill and integrity will bring to the door of a man who begins with nothing but these qualities as his capital. For the finest work done in the most artistic manner, this house is famed, as it is done directly and entirely under the supervision of Mr. Pekor himself, their work proving as guaranteed. It is a pleasure to point out Mr. Pekor as a self-made man, whose success is notable.

U. H. SMITH—Druggist, and Dealer in Fancy and Toilet Articles of every Description, Tobacco and Cigars, Garden Seeds and Lamps, Phenix City, Ala.

There is no other nation which so fully appreciates the value, or makes such intelligent use of drugs and chemical preparations, as the people of the South: nor is there any nation on earth where so high a degree of intelligence and thorough comprehension of their individual properties and virtues is required for the prosecution of this important branch of trade, which may be appropriately classified as both an industrial and commercial pursuit. Entitled to favorable consideration in a review of the representative establishments of Phenix City the well-known house of U. H. Smith demands more than ordinary consideration in this connection. Pioneers, not only in their special lines of trade, but in business energy, commercial progress and industrial endeavor, the history of these staunch old houses makes the material for the biographies of cities, landmarks in the book of time illustrating the growth and progress of mercantile interest. Such a history has the drug store of U. H. Smith, established in 1883—and now claims a prominent rank among its contemporaries in every sense of the term—a first-class and reliable pharmacy for the preparation of physician's prescriptions. Mr. Smith is a thoroughly educated druggist and pharmacist, having devoted twenty years of his life to the study of the details of his business in all of its branches. He carries an extensive stock of pure medicines, drugs and chemicals, together with a full line of toilet articles, perfumes, powders, extracts, choice soaps, brushes, sponges, and a large assortment of everything legitimately included in his line of business. Next door to his drug store is the U. H. Smith Furniture Company, composed of Messrs. U. H. Smith, L. T. Jones and E. A. Albright—all men of sterling business qualities. This house was established in 1888 by the above firm. They at once recognized the fact that the dealers who were up to the progress of the age were the most prosperous and most successful in satisfying the demands of the trade. Hence they purchased a complete stock of the most desirable articles in that line, embracing an extensive and varied display of fine and plain furniture—from the elaborate and costly to the plain and inexpensive styles. Parlor, bed-room, dining-room, library, office and kitchen furniture in all styles and prices. The men in charge of this department having a number of years experience, combined with ability, intelligence and honest square dealings have made their business a success, and we heartily commend them to our readers.

POWER'S CASH STORE—PHENIX CITY, ALA.

In preparing a comprehensive work on the commerce and industries of a city, we often meet with men who have had such wonderful success that we pause and wonder if they were not born "under some lucky star," and we take especial delight in informing the many readers of our work of the success these firms have attained. In this connection we desire to make mention of "Power's Cash Store," dealer in confectioneries, cigars and tobacco, making a specialty of goobers. He sells more goobers than any house in Columbus. The phenomenal success of Mr. Power is not due, however, to any "lucky star," but to his integrity and honest business principles, together with industry and enterprise. He also carries a large stock of fruits, nuts, etc., ice cream and cold drinks in season. Mr. Power is a native of Savannah, Ga., and has only been here for nine months, but since he first opened has done an excellent business. We heartily commend him to our readers.

DR. D. E. MORGAN—SPECIFIC REMEDY CO., OF THE BRITISH SCHOOLS, SOUTH WALES, ENG., REMEDIES FOR ALL CHRONIC AND FEMALE DISEASES, PHENIX CITY, ALA.

The drug store of Dr. D. E. Morgan, Phenix City, Ala., occupies a prominent position among the leading houses in this line, and as well for the ample qualifications associated in its management as the excellent location, has secured a liberal patronage from the medical profession and citizens. He carries a complete stock of pure drugs, medicines and chemicals, besides perfumeries, toilet articles, choice cigars and tobacco. Dr. Morgan is a native of England, and a graduate of the South Wales British schools. He makes a specialty of remedies for chronic and female diseases and cancer; particularly cancer, for which he has a never-failing remedy. By enclosing a two-cent stamp to any of the following names you can get any information desired regarding the cure:

Mrs. Duncan, Phenix City, Ala.: Mrs. Lamb, Crawford, Ala.: Mrs. Russ, Griffin, Ga.: Mrs. Rogers, Phenix City, Ala.; Mrs. C. Morris, Salt Lake, Ala.

Read the following and we think you will be convinced:

VERY REMARKABLE.

Mr. Moses M. Harvey, of Columbus, Ga., has been suffering for a period of ten years from a rose cancer, and after trying all the leading physicians of Columbus, and being pronounced incurable, he gave up all hopes of recovery and became resigned to his sad fate. By chance he heard of a remarkable cure being accomplished by Dr. Morgan, formerly of England, and like a drowning man grasping at a straw he at once sought this now famous doctor, and after a consultation he decided to give the doctor an opportunity to test his remedy, and in just two weeks the cancer was removed from his neck, and now he is fully cured, although at the time the cancer was removed his neck was almost eaten through. The cancer is now in a bottle at Dr. Morgan's Drug Store, Phenix City, Ala.

PHENIX CITY, ALA.

Before me, L. Booker, Justice of the Peace for Beat 10, Lee county, personally came Moses M. Harvey, of Columbus, Ga., who, being duly sworn, deposeth and saith that the above statements are true. MOSES M. HARVEY.

Sworn to and subscribed before me November 12th, 1891.

L. BOOKER, J. P.

WM. A. WIMBISH—ATTORNEY AT LAW.

There is no city in the South better provided with brilliant legal talent than Columbus, and no city where those engaged in the practice of law stand higher in the social scale. In this connection we desire to mention the name of Mr. Wm. A. Wimbish as a lawyer of sterling business qualities, who has the confidence of his fellowman, not only for his ability as a legal adviser, but for his high integrity, industry and business qualifications. Mr. Wimbish is a native Georgian, born in LaGrange in 1859, and graduating with the highest honors at Washington Lee University in 1878; has been practicing in this city for nearly five years with much success, both legally and financially. Such men go far towards making a prosperous and thrifty city. We take pleasure in commending him to our readers at home or abroad as a prompt, reliable and energetic lawyer, who will attend promptly and properly to all business placed in his hands.

S. J. ROGERS—PHOTOGRAPHER, 1010½ BROAD STREET.

Boucicault, in his popular play of "The Octoroon," brings down the house by making Salem Scudder say to Simon Legree, when confronted with the proof of his guilt in the picture obtained from the camera, "The instrument never lies!" This clever melo-dramatist's touch elicits applause, but with all due deference to his dramatic ability we differ with him, or rather with the sentiment there expressed, as a bad disposition or posing of the subject; imperfect and injudicious lighting and bad development may not only totally destroy the likeness, but render beauty sometime hideous. This is, however, avoided by the operator who thoroughly understands his business, and who, possessed of the artistic element in his training, will so pose his sitter and adjust the lights and surroundings as to develop into prominence all the beauty and desirable points, and also communicate charms which they hardly may be said to ordinarily possess. Pictures are satisfactory or otherwise, according to the measures of his artistic ability and skill; and who has not been charmed by a really fine photograph and disgusted by its opposite? These reflections are the result of the pleasure derived from a thorough inspection of Mr. Rogers' specimens, which are so perfect in every essential of fine photography that we can hardly restrain and limit our praise and commendation. Mr. Rogers first entered this business in 1866, and has done a successful business since 1868. His studio is located 1010½ Broad street, formerly occupied by A. J. Riddle, who established the place in 1852, Mr. Rogers succeeding him in May of this year. He is a Virginian by birth, and has brought with him to his adopted home all the gentlemanly attributes for which those of his native State are so well known. Mr. Rogers is a courteous and refined gentleman, a consummate artist, and has for a motto, elegance, accuracy, and last, though not least, punctuality.

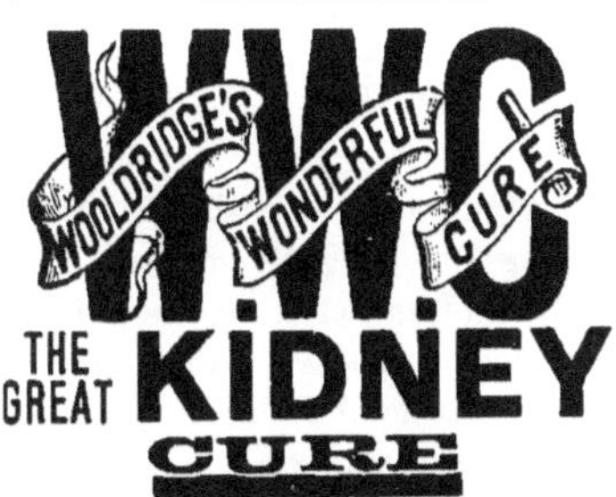

The reputation of this wonder extends that of the city in which it is manufactured, the success attendant upon the efforts of the W. W. C. Co. has been phenomenal, and it is with pride that our citizens can point out the fact that the home office of this great product is in Columbus. So, also, is it the home of its officers and stockholders, among whom are the leading citizens. Mr. L. F. Humber, of Blanchard, Humber & Co., warehouse and commission merchants, is the President, and Mr. J. R. Garrett, for twenty years in the cotton business, is the Secretary and Treasurer. Mr. T. E. Blanchard, President of the Fourth National Bank, is one of the largest stockholders. Mr. Albert Wooldridge, the discoverer of the W. W. C., is one of our leading cotton merchants. He formerly lived in Chattahoochee county, and it was there he manufactured W. W. C. on a small scale, and in a charitable and Christian spirit distributed gratis, more medicine than was sold, and so wonderful were the cures effected, that the reputation of W. W. C. was above par with those who came in contact with it, and in 1889 a party of capitalists here readily took up the necessary stock to have this medicine put before the world, hence, the W. W. C. Co. of Columbus. The sales of this Company in 1891 was 300,000 bottles, this output being distributed throughout the Southern and Western States, and some to the City of Mexico. This Company issues a challenge to the world, offering a reward of $1,000 for any case of blood poison that the W. W. C. will not cure. Not an instance is on record wherein this medicine has failed to perform the functions for which it was intended. Testimonials from reputable citizens here are in reach of any one desiring to fully acquaint themselves with its great value. Mr. John R. Garrett, the Secretary, is ever glad to furnish a list of names of those who have profited by the use of W. W. C. The Company having been so fortunate in making large sales of their blood purifier, the W. W. C., have decided to manufacture other medicines of superior formulas. These are, pills, cough syrup, diarrhœa mixture, worm candy, linament and arromatic tonic. The splendid management of Mr. J. R. Garrett in putting out the blood medicine insures a bright future for the entire list. The Company is to be congratulated upon their success, and for the benefit they have done to suffering humanity in relieving thousands of living beings, who would otherwise to-day have been in their graves.

J. H. CONNOR & CO.—Dealers in Staple Dry Goods and Groceries, 1023 Broad Street.

The reputation and commercial claims of a city centre in the character of its representative business institutions, and, in the historical review of the industries and enterprises of a community, those establishments of acknowledged merit and true mercantile ability are considered important component parts, worthy of critical description and justifiable pride. Among the establishments which have materially contributed to the fame of Columbus as a commercial centre, possessing undoubted advantages and facilities and adding to the general progress of the community, the house of J. H. Connor & Co. claims a decided recognition. Messrs. J. H. Connor and William McGovern commenced business here in August, 1865, with fair capital, which close attention, thorough knowledge of the business, energetic, prompt mercantile habits and liberal principles has largely increased. The business premises of this firm consist of a lot 35x125 feet in size, with a building 35x100 feet located upon it, giving them certain facilities for handling goods that can be appreciated by those conversant with this line of business. The stock is large and well selected, including staple dry goods and groceries, crockery, glass, tin, wood and hollow-ware, the value reaching, if not exceeding, $10,000. The trade supplied is local, including the city and country contiguous, and the annual transactions will reach $50,000. New supplies are being constantly received, and in every respect this is a most satisfactory house to visit for supplies. Mr. J. H. Connor came here from Ireland in 1848, and Mr. William McGovern came to Columbus in 1853. They have done, and are doing a prosperous and steadily increasing business, retaining their trade by fair and honorable treatment of each customer.

C. L. TORBETT—Undertaker and Practical Embalmer, 930 and 932 Broad.

Ever since the year 1878 the name of C. L. Torbett has been familiar to the people of Columbus, and a more successful undertaker than he has never entered into the somewhat grave, though important, business of preparing caskets for the reception of the remains of mortality. His factory, salesroom and wareroom are located at 930 and 932 Broad street. His storeroom occupies 40x60 feet, salesroom 30x60 feet, paint room 15x16, and his work-shop 15x45, affording ample room for a number of workmen, and within its walls are constantly being made coffins of every description. Mr. Torbett is thoroughly posted in all the details of his business. He managed successfully for five years the embalming and undertaker department for L. Rooney. He then bought out Mr. Rooney, taking Mr. Coleman in as a partner in 1883. The business then flourished under the name of Coleman & Torbett until 1885, at which time Mr. Torbett bought out Mr. Coleman, giving him the exclusive control of the business, and under his management he has built up a trade second to none in the city. His stock is complete, embracing the latest and newest styles of coffins, caskets and ornaments, screws and all fixtures used in the business. Mr. Torbett has a thorough knowledge of embalming, and keeps himself posted right up in all the details and branches pertaining to it. He is a native Georgian, and is a gentleman possessed of many generous qualities, and is widely known for his high integrity and business qualifications. He is strictly temperate and attentive to business, a genial, whole-souled gentleman, who will make you feel welcome whenever you enter his house, and in his absence you will find his clever and gentlemanly assistant, Mr. F. C. Rummel ever ready to extend the same cordial greeting. Mr. Torbett has officiated on very important occasions at the obsequies of prominent public men. He has filled honorably all the high offices of the secret orders to which he belongs, and is a member of the Columbus Athletic Club. Mr. Torbett has furnished the city with all their embalming and undertaker's work since 1886, thus proving the satisfactory manner in which he does his work. He is always ready to meet any emergency, and we heartily recommend him to the public.

W. H. YOUNG CO.—MANUFACTURERS OF PANTALOONS, JEANS SUITS, SHIRTS, OVERALLS, JACKETS, ETC.

The above represents one of the new industries of Columbus. One great benefit to a community resulting from the manufacture of clothing, is the immense field of employment it opens up for females. Our city has, for a number of years, enjoyed a wide reputation as an extensive cotton manufacturing point, and added to this, is fast developing into a prominent jeans and clothing manufacturing city, the grade and product of this last mentioned branch being of such high class as to attract considerable notice with the trade; and among the finest equipped establishments is the W. H. Young Co., which was incorporated in 1891, with C. L. Perkins, President: A. C. Young, Secretary and Treasurer; and J. W. Boyd, Superintendent. Mr. Perkins came here from Chicago, where he for a number of years represented several of the largest mills in the South, and having a knowledge of the advantages of Columbus, decided to cast his lot here. Mr. A. C. Young needs no introduction to the trade of the South, his long term of office with the Eagle and Phenix Manufacturing Company bringing him within communication of the leading merchants of the country, and by his great business enterprise and integrity has established an enviable reputation. Mr. J. W.

COLUMBUS

TRADE MARK

Boyd is a king as a manager; fifteen years with the leading clothing factories of the West, has familiarized him with every detail of the business in which he is engaged, and in securing the outfit for the W. H. Young Co., he made it a point to procure every known improvement in the system of cutting, trimming, and making of garments, hence the advantages of this plant in turning out superior made clothing, which is resulting in a surprisingly active demand for their product. When the entire machinery is fitted up, and the business gets under headway, the trade will amount to a quarter of a million dollars per annum. Columbus has cause to be proud of this institution.

MILES & LOTT—General Agents Penn Mutual Life Insurance Co.

A life insurance company may be proprietary, mutual or mixed. A mutual company is an association of persons, each of whom is an insurer as well as insured. Policy holders exercise control through their votes for managers, and are entitled to all the profits or dividends of the society. Policies of insurance are of various kinds. The chief of them are: whole life, endowment, endowment assurance, term, joint life, annuity and survivorship annuity. Other varieties are obtained from these by modification or combination of conditions. A purely mutual company is the Penn Mutual Life Insurance Company, of Philadelphia, Pa., which was incorporated in 1847, and whose charter is perpetual. It is most ably represented in Columbus by Messrs. Miles & Lott, who established their office here in 1891 and do a large local business, as well as an extensive business throughout Southwest Georgia, embracing some of the best cities in the State. No prudent man will fail to leave his family in good circumstances at death, when it can be so easily done by a systematic payment of a small sum to the party who contracts to pay the sum total at his death. In all portions of the United States the Penn Mutual is regarded as a stable and trustworthy company. Messrs. G. G. Miles and W. L. Lott compose the firm. Mr. Miles is a son of the late Rev. Thos. J. Miles, who spent nearly fifty years preaching the Baptist faith in Georgia and Alabama. In the early part of 1861 Mr. Miles moved with his father's family to Montgomery county, Ala., where he followed agricultural pursuits, and in the meantime received only a high school education. In 1878 he left the farm and moved to the city of Montgomery, Ala., where he engaged in the lumber business with marked success. In the fall of 1879 he had a flattering offer made him by an elder brother to engage in the mercantile business in Birmingham, Ala., which he accepted and followed for seven years, building up an immense trade. Having previously led an active outdoor life, the store and counting room did not agree with him, so he sold out his interest in the store and engaged in the real estate and insurance business, which proved equally as successful as former pursuits. In the spring of 1891 he moved back to his old native State, locating in Columbus, where he accepted, in conjunction with Mr. W. L. Lott, the general agency for the Penn Mutual Life for Southwest Georgia. Mr. Miles, having had a number of year's experience in the insurance business, and Mr. Lott being a man of superior business tact, and representing one of the strongest and most reliable companies, is no matter of surprise that their first year's business has been crowned with phenominal success. Mr. Lott was born in Clay county, Ga., in 1855. The early part of his life was spent on the farm, where he received a good high school education, and afterwards turned his attention to commercial marts, and in 1882 moved to Columbus and accepted a position as head bookkeeper for the well-known establishment of J. A. Kirven & Co. The success of this firm is due largely to Mr. Lott's untiring energy and careful handling of the accounts and finances. With the marked success which has already attended this firm the past year, and as they represent one of the strongest and best known companies for honest and square dealing in the United States, we not only bespeak for them a successful career in the future, but we can cheerfully add that those who place their insurance in Penn Mutual Life make a wise selection, as is evidenced by the satisfaction always given to policy holders, both in dividend earnings and prompt settlements.

VERANDA HOTEL—W. H. GIBSON, PROPRIETOR, CORNER FIRST AVENUE AND TENTH STREET.

In making mention of the hotels of this city and studying the phases of hotel life, our attention is drawn to the fact that as the tastes and means of people widely differ, so must this branch of business vary, in order to meet all the requirements of the great traveling public. With this point in view we desire to call attention to the Veranda Hotel; it is located convenient to all branches of business, on corner First avenue and Tenth street, one block from Broad. This hotel contains fifteen bedrooms, a large, commodious dining-room, convenient to office and all parts of the house, with 150 feet of front veranda's, from which a very fine view of both business and resident part of the city can be had. All who wish to procure good permanent or transient board, at moderate prices, will find this house to meet their desires in every respect. Mr. W. H. Gibson assumed control of this hotel October 1891, and since has made many improvements, and his success in its management has been such as to insure him a liberal patronage for the future. Mr. Gibson is a native of Alabama, born in Macon county, where he spent his early life. Later in life he entered the general merchanchise business at Mott's Mills, Ala., where he conducted successfully his business till 1890: then moving to this city he secured a position on the police force, which he very satisfactorily fills at present. Mr. Gibson is a man of high standing, strictly sober and attentive to business, doing justice to all, he has become well-known and esteemed by all who know him. To our readers and traveling public generally we commend the Veranda Hotel.

EXCELSIOR STEAM LAUNDRY—PEASE BROTHERS, PROPRIETORS, 1211 BROAD STREET.

Among the many industries that tend to make a town metropolitan, none work with greater force toward this end than the steam laundry. A few years ago the "Heathen Chinee" came with his craft and took away the labor from the washer woman, and now the laundry run by steam, with patent washer, starching machine, ironer, and heat dryer, has almost entirely suppressed the

Celestial as the American washer, where five or ten years ago the Mongolian held sway with "No ticket no washee." The lightning working steam machinery has taken his place, and in many sections he is as great a curiosity as he was before he made his advent. Christian invention, with the aid of steam, has taken his occupation as he took the occupation of the patient females of our own blood. In 1888 Columbus, always alive to progress, established the Excelsior Steam Laundry at 1211 Broad street, where, from the first, it has taken the lead in this section for the class of work turned out, and the rapidity with which it was executed. In 1891 Messrs. Pease Bros. bought out the stock company, and have since that time conducted the business in the same satisfactory manner, increasing the trade weekly. The laundry is fitted out with the latest improved laundry machinery, which is driven by a 10-horse power engine and 14-horse power boiler. They occupy a floor space of 40x200 feet, and give employment to nine people. Mr. E. L. Pease, the manager, is a gentleman of high social standing, having many warm friends here. He is a young man of no ordinary ability, as his success shows.

H. L. WARE—"The Hustler," Dry Goods, Notions, Shoes and Gents' Furnishings, No. 1007 Broad Street.

In enumerating the industries of a city there are certain controlling staples which exercise a vital influence upon its reputation and trade, and no one business occupies this position more prominently than the dry goods trade, and none offers greater inducements to the enterprising business man for the investment of capital, while there is no branch of trade where popular talents contribute more largely to success than the dry goods store, where patronage depends so much upon public favor. Among the establishments in Columbus who have evidenced the possession of these qualifications in a marked degree none stand higher in public estimation than Mr. H. L. Ware. This house was established by the firm of Ware & Bohannon, Mr. Ware being sole proprietor at the present time. It was started with ample capital and energy, industry and enterprise, and a natural adaptability to the business soon attracted and held a remunerative trade. With honesty of purpose and due consideration for the welfare of their customers, which is the true foundation of good business principles, this house has become popular wherever known. A full and complete stock of dry goods, notions, shoes and gents' furnishing goods is carried, valued at $5,000. The store-room occupied is 25x70 feet in size and well adapted to the display of goods. A large local trade is supplied, the sales reaching $25,000, and three assistants are employed, Mr. Ware also giving personal attention to sales. The stock will be found, both in quality and selection, equal to that of any house in the city. Mr. Ware is a native Georgian—an energetic, active business man—thoroughly conversant with his business, and justly merits the esteem and confidence of the business community and trade generally.

A. G. RHODES FURNITURE CO.—DEALERS IN ALL STYLES AND GRADES OF FURNITURE. JOBBING A SPECIALTY—1029 BROAD STREET.

Within the last decade, the manufacture of furniture and cabinet making have greatly advanced in this country. The Southern demand, which is proverbially fastidious in the selection of furniture, is dependent on the North and

COLUMBUS LEDGER ENG.

West for a large portion of their supply, with increasing demand. There has been a corresponding improvement of taste in design, and nowhere can there be exhibited a finer display than can be seen at the spacious furniture house of The

A. G. Rhodes Furniture Company, at 1029 Broad street. In this special line of industrial enterprise there is no house in the city or State better known or more entitled to recognition in a work that assumes to make a complete and exhaustive exhibit of the commercial resources of the city. The building occupied by The A. G. Rhodes Furniture Company is commodious and convenient, being 145 x 30 feet and four stories. Sixteen employees are engaged in conducting the large business transacted by this house, their wholesale trade reaching throughout this State, Alabama and Florida, which gives Columbus a prestige as a wholesale furniture market. The average amount of stock carried is about $25,000, this being continually replenished as sales are made. The annual sales foot up to about $100,000. The officers of this company are A. G. Rhodes, of Atlanta, President; W. J. Smith, of Atlanta, Vice-President, and T. F. Smith, of Columbus, Ga., Secretary and Treasurer. The President of the company, Mr. A. G. Rhodes, is more extensively interested in the furniture business than any other man in the entire South, being connected with eighteen different houses in as many prominent Southern points, among which are Louisville, Ky., Nashville, Tenn., Memphis, Atlanta, Charleston, S. C., Savannah, Ga., Evansville, Ind., Cairo, Ill., etc. The business here is in charge of Mr. T. F. Smith, the Secretary and Treasurer, who began the study of the furniture business about eighteen years ago, and has demonstrated that he is thorough in this line by establishing here and taking the lead over every other house in the city much older than his. Mr. Smith is one of our shrewd and wide-awake business men, and a most desirable citizen. He will continue to steer the business of the A. G. Rhodes Furniture Company on to success, keeping in the lead of every other craft that might be in the race with him.

"CREOLE" PILE CURE.

Among the many industries which have had their beginning in Columbus, none have merited more, nor succeeded better, for the past few months of its existence, than the manufacturers of "Creole" Pile Cure. This remedy has proved to be an absolute specific for piles and hemorrhoids of all kinds, fistula in ano, ulcerated womb or vagina, granulated eyelids, opthalmia and sore eyes, old sores and ulcers, ulcerated rectum, acute or chronic dysentery or diarrhea, itch, chillblain or frost bite, curing in a few hours or days, without pain or detention from business, any of these diseases, it matters not of how long standing, after all other treatment has failed. The price of the medicine is $5 per full package delivered to you with guarantee to cure any of the above diseases, or trial packages 60 cents by mail. The general agent, Mr. E. A. Shiver, to whom all orders should be addressed, states that he has sold upwards of three thousand full packages to parties all over the country, with not a solitary dissenter from the universal verdict. The medicine is endorsed by some of the leading citizens of Columbus and elsewhere, who have been cured by using it, when everything else had failed. If you wish to get cured, try it.

FRAZER HOUSE—Mrs. C. B. Frazer, Proprietress, 924 and 926 Broad.

Situated in a most convenient and pleasant part of the city, this hotel is a most desirable stopping place for all who wish the best accommodations and attention at the most reasonable rates. Its corps of servants are well disciplined and attentive, and the tables are supplied with all the delicacies of the season.

The office, parlor and dining room are on the first floor, and the next story for bed rooms exclusively. Every attention is paid to the guests, and no pains are spared to make it in all respects one of the best in the city. Mrs. Frazer, proprietress, is well known and esteemed, and her long and varied experience peculiarly fits her for the present position.

Before Operation.

After Operation.

Note.—The successful termination of this case has caused no little interest with the leading opthalmologists in the United States and Europe.

DR. W. L. BULLARD Occulist and Aurist.

In order to give a full and complete statistical statement of the industries of Columbus, such as this volume is intended to contain, it is necessary to include all the industrial arts and professions, as well as the commercial interest. There can be no question as to the validity of the claims of the profession of a physician to be specially represented in this work. This profession is one which operates effectively in time of need, in arresting and alleviating the most acute pains and ailments to which the human body is heir, and therefore deserves the most thankful and appreciative consideration on the part of the public. We consider the man who prepares a preparation to cure the eye, ear, throat or nose of his fellow men and women, a public benefactor, who deserves well of the people. Dr. Bullard is a native Georgian, and has had a number of years' experience, taking his first course in Maryland University, and graduated in medicine in Atlanta, 1877. He at once began the practice of his profession at Tennille, Ga., and enjoyed a large and extensive practice there till 1882, at which time he moved to Columbus, and remained here only a few months before going to New York, in the private office of Dr. W. W. Mittendorf. He also attended courses at the New York Eye and Ear Hospital, and then at Polyclinic, going from there to London, where he graduated at the London Opthalmic Hospital. He also studied at Dr. Morrell McKinzie's hospital for throat and chest. He then visited hospitals in Atrech, Holland, and Vienna, Austria, returning to Columbus in 1884, practicing exclusively on the eye, ear, throat and nose diseases since. Since his advent here, he has gained an enviable position in the city, both as a practitioner and business man. He is always active in everything that tends to the advancement of the commerce of our city. He is a gentleman of superior ability, as a physician he has few equals, and as a citizen he is an honor to his native State.

COLUMBUS INVESTMENT COMPANY.

"The busy world throws angrily aside the man who stands with arms akimbo set, until occasion tells him what to do."

The earnest workers of Columbus are too energetic to wait for the occasion but promptly *make* it. Appreciating the advantages offered by Columbus as a home, and convinced that many who now pay rent would gladly own their own homes if they had the means, or could borrow on long time at a reasonable rate of interest, a number of our far-sighted and progressive citizens in May 1889 organized the Columbus Investment Company with a capital stock of $100,000 subscribed, and in June of that year with $2,000 paid in they began business. Their purpose, the upbuilding and development of Columbus, has been followed to the letter. In the past three years they have aided in the erection of and built for themselves and others over one hundred handsome houses. The Company has now a subscribed capital stock of $250,000 with $195,000 paid in, the balance maturing at the rate of $5,000 monthly.

They have paid the stockholders three handsome cash dividends, have a nice surplus, and have loaned over $200,000 on city property. We are of the opinion that no better showing can be made by any Investment, Loan or Building Association. This Company is established on a purely business basis with a liberal charter which gives them ample opportunity to earn money legitimately and still give the borrower low rates of interest.

This Company is now contemplating the erection of a handsome office building on the corner of Twelfth street and First avenue, immediately opposite the lot recently purchased by the Government for a United States court and Post-office building. If built in accordance with the preliminary plans and sketches made it will prove an ornament to the city and reflect great credit on the Company.

The Board of Directors consist of the following well-known, practical and successful business men, each of whose names will be found identified with almost every move which has been made in recent years for the material advancement of Columbus. They each and all give to the Company's affairs their close personal attention, which accounts in a large measure for the great success of the Company :

Officers- Jno. F. Flournoy, President; G. W. McElhaney, Vice-President; Chas. M. Woolfolk, Secretary and Treasurer.

Directors—Jno. F. Flournoy, T. M. Foley, Jas. P. Kyle, I. Joseph, Jas. K. Orr, H. L. Woodruff, G. W. McElhaney, H. H. Epping, jr., Luther Frazer, L. F. Garrard, M. E. Gray, N. P. Banks, Soule Redd, of Columbus, Ga.; Herman Myers, Geo. J. Baldwin, of Savannah, Ga.

Auditing Committee, by whom the books and vouchers of the Company are audited each month—Sam Salisbury, A. S. Mason, L. Meyer.

E. JUNGERMAN—Photographic Studio, 1011½ Broad Street.

The vast progress in the photographic art since the days of Daguerre, and its wonderful culmination in the science of the present day, is vividly illustrated by a visit to the gallery of Mr. E. Jungerman, who has but recently engaged in business in our city. His rooms are located at 1011½ Broad street, upstairs, which is a central location, and the latest improved appliances are used, thus ensuring good workmanship. Mr. Jungerman was born in Germany, and commenced the study of this art thirteen years ago, coming to this city in 1891. His thorough and practical education has been greatly in his favor, as he at once took a leading position as an artist of true merit, and from the start he has been successful. He has given particular attention throughout his long experience to light and shade and the art of position, and his work is unequaled in its truth to nature and in exquisite finish. His positions are characterized by ease and grace and his results invariably satisfactory. Every style of photographic work is done in a surprising style and upon liberal terms, and a very complete and perfect assortment of photographic instruments, appendages and stock is kept on hand, prompt attention being given to all orders entrusted to him. Mr. Jungerman solicits a share of the public patronage, confident that he can give entire satisfaction to all.

HILL, REESE & CO.—Real Estate and Insurance.

The place occupied by the firm of Messrs. Hill, Reese & Co. in this community is such that, in compiling the commercial, manufacturing and other advantages of Columbus, our work would be incomplete were we to omit mention of a house which adds to the solvency and solidity of its operations by means of experience and reliability in its special line of transactions. The business of handling real estate has become a great factor in the transactions of the world's business, and its uses are becoming the better recognized since its mutual utility has been discovered. It is a distinct business, in the prosecution of which not only superior business ability is requisite, but a thorough knowledge of values, unquestioned probity and untiring energy. Applying these positive tests, the house of Messrs. Hill, Reese & Co. must be recognized as the representative real estate agency in Columbus. These gentlemen have on their books an extensive list of city property, also acreage property lying adjacent to the city, and correspondence is solicited from outside parties wishing to make good, safe investments. Messrs. J. B. Hill, George Reese and D. R. Allen compose the firm, all gentlemen of marked ability in this line of business. Mr. Hill has been engaged in this line here for a number of years, and has a thorough knowledge of the value of property located in various parts of the city. They are prepared to transact any amount of business in the insurance department, and no firm can offer better inducements for the accomplishment of any business entrusted to them. The office is situated at No. 19 West Eleventh street, between Front and Broad.

W. J. GREEN—Boot and Shoe Maker, 930 Broad Street.

The subject of this sketch, Mr. W. J. Green, is one of the leading men in this city in the manufacture and repairing of boots and shoes. He is thoroughly posted in his business, serving two years as cutter in the war, besides an apprenticeship of five years under Wm. Myers. Seeing the necessity of time and labor saving machines, Mr. Green turned his attention to the invention of a skiving board, which he has used successfully for a long time, proving it to be very valuable in repairing and manufacturing shoes, etc. Mr. Green makes a specialty of repairing, and gets a sufficiency to keep him busy all the time, thus proving the style and durability of his work. Mr. Green is a native of Montgomery, Ala., where he was born in 1838. He came to Columbus in 1862, and has since made himself a fair and honorable name among our best people. With his accustomed thrift, he has created a good business and made his sterling qualities felt in the community, and is in every way deserving of a generous support.

ROBT. DAVIS & CO.—Dealers in Groceries, Liquors, Cigars, Tobaccos, Etc., 1431 First Avenue.

In the preparation of this work, the contents of which are designed to convey to the reader some idea of the business capabilities, industrial resources and commercial relations of our city, it has been our aim to present to the consideration of the public only such firms and establishments as may be justly regarded active elements in advancing the general prosperity of the city of Columbus. In pursuit of this aim, we call attention to the house of Robt. Davis & Co., dealers in groceries, liquors, cigars, tobacco, etc., at No. 1431 First avenue. This firm commenced business in 1883 with a moderate capital, and have gained a liberal patronage, with satisfactory increase in business. They carry a stock of about $5,000 in value, which is kept in excellent order and condition, and they are in frequent receipt of fresh goods, keeping the stock thoroughly replenished with the freshest and best class of articles for home and table use. The trade is general through the surrounding country, Georgia and Alabama, and reaches $32,000 per annum. Three assistants are employed, who serve their many patrons with the various articles to be found in this establishment, including family and fancy groceries, flour, coffees, teas, sugars, soaps, candles, etc., besides a general assortment of sundries, in fact, almost every article entering into family consumption; also a specialty is made of plantation supplies. They occupy two store-rooms, which are 50x60 feet in extent, and the shelving and counters are loaded with as choice a selection of goods as can be found in the city and at as popular prices. The firm is composed of Messrs. Robert Davis and Rollin Jefferson, both natives of this State, who have had some years experience in this line of business. They are reliable, energetic and trustworthy, and have established an enviable business reputation, entitling them to a high position among the business men of Columbus.

A. H. GINSBERG—Wholesale and Retail Dealer in Gents' Furnishing Goods, Notions, Clothing, Shoes, Etc., Watches and Jewelry a Specialty, 1230 Broad Street.

Among the large number of commercial houses which honor and dignify the name of Columbus, we find none more worthy of favorable mention than that whose name stands at the head of this article. It was started in 1889 with but limited capital, and now a large and well selected stock is exhibited. As an experienced buyer, the proprietor, Mr. Ginsberg, is enabled to select those articles best suited to the various tastes shown by customers. Gents' furnishing goods of expensive or the cheaper qualities may be obtained here, notions of every description, a large assortment of clothing, shoes and other articles in this line, and a specialty is made of watches and jewelry. A store-room 18x90 feet in size is fully occupied, and several employees are in constant attendance. Mr. Ginsberg was born in Russia in 1857, and commenced his mercantile career in 1875. On arriving in our city he opened up this business for himself, and is fast gaining a high place in the esteem of this community.

B. ROTHSCHILD Dry Goods, Clothing, Boots, Shoes, Hats, Etc., 1216 and 1218 Broad Street.

One of the most enterprising and thorough-going business men in that section of the city is Mr. B. Rothschild, dealer in dry goods, clothing, boots, shoes, hats, etc. His is the leading establishment in that section, and meritoriously enjoys the patronage of the best class of citizens. This trade, considered as a branch of commerce, is the most important of any now existing within the city's limits. It controls an immense amount of capital, employs a small army of people, and distributes a greater amount of commodities than any other branch of mercantile pursuits. Mr. Rothschild opened business here in 1885, and since that time has received a very encouraging support. He started with small capital, which his energy, industry and practical ability soon increased and secured him a remunerative and steadily growing trade. The stock includes everything necessary for the outfit of man, woman or child, from head to foot, of expensive or cheaper quality, as may be desired, and is valued at $10,000.

Several assistants are employed, who are courteous and affable to all who may call in quest of goods in this line. The trade is generally local, and will reach $30,000 per annum. The store-room occupied is 35x90 feet in size, and well adapted to the display of goods of every description. Mr. Rothschild was born in Merchingen, Germany, but has resided in Columbus for ten years past. He has had twelve years experience in the dry goods and clothing trade, and is well prepared to understand the wants of his patrons. The length of time this establishment has been engaged in business, and the well known honorable basis upon which all its transactions have been conducted, has won for its proprietor a reputation to which nothing further need be added or required.

WM. REDD, JR.—REAL ESTATE AND FIRE INSURANCE AGENT, NO. 1047 BROAD STREET.

The most essential qualifications for the successful prosecution of the real estate business in the principal cities of the Union, in addition to a thorough knowledge of values, is a keen discrimination and a strict regard for truth and honor in all transactions, since through the representations of agents large investments are made involving immense sums of money. Mr. William Redd, Jr., possesses in an eminent degree the qualifications we have enumerated above, and his name is familiar in business circles as one of our most successful, conscientious citizens. The facilities enjoyed by him in the handling of valuable real estate, both in the city and country, are unsurpassed, and much desirable property, both improved and unimproved, is found under his control. Mr. Redd engaged in this business the first of last year, and from the start has been popular and successful. He has now on hand a large number of investments, offering superior inducements, both of city real estate and farm lands. Mr. Redd was born in LaGrange, Ga., but has resided in Columbus most of his life—hence is well known to our residents. He possesses the confidence of our people, and is held in the highest respect as among our first citizens and business men. Some of the very best and strongest fire insurance companies are represented by him, and he is prepared to issue policies without delay. By his activity, energy and prompt business characteristics, he has won for himself a high business reputation.

J. JOSEPH—DEALER IN STAPLE AND FANCY DRY GOODS, CLOTHING, BOOTS, SHOES, HATS AND TRUNKS, 1102 BROAD STREET.

In recording any adequate account of the industries of Columbus, and the progress made during the last quarter of a century in commercial and manufacturing importance, it would be impossible to omit mention of the house of Mr. J. Joseph. Established by the present owner in 1868, the resources and trade of this concern have more than kept pace with the general prosperity of the city. Founded with but limited capital, but conducted with every advantage to be derived from a stainless business policy, the success of the house increased with each succeeding year, until at the present time it stands on a very solid basis.

Mr. Joseph occupies the commodious three-story building, 24x75 feet in size, located at No. 1102 Broad street, where is displayed a well selected and most desirable assortment of staple and fancy dry goods, clothing, boots and shoes, hats and trunks, valued at $15,000. Several assistants are employed to attend to customers, and Mr. Joseph gives his personal attention to the business. Customers patronizing this enterprise are residents of Georgia and Alabama in this vicinity, and the annual transactions will reach $25,000 to $30,000. Mr. Joseph was born in Germany in 1845, commenced operations in this line of business in 1864, and engaged in business here three years later. He is a man of large acquaintance in business circles, and his reputation as an upright business man is second to none in this city.

GRIGSBY E. THOMAS, JR.—Attorney and Counsellor at Law, Rooms 3 and 4, Second Floor, Georgia Home Building.

In the preparation of these sketches of business and professional men the object is to preserve, in some way, the biographies of our citizens, and we could not call the work complete did we fail to make mention of those men who were born in Muscogee county and spent their lives in developing this section. Mr. Thomas was born on Rose Hill, Columbus, Ga., September 7, 1842. After serving four years in the Confederate army he began the practice of law, succeeding his father, the late Judge G. E. Thomas, who died July 5, 1865. He now practices in all the courts of this State and Texas. When the State of Texas declared her Independence of Mexico in 1835-36, and appealed for volunteers, Mirabeau B. Lamar, then editor and proprietor of the Columbus Enquirer, espoused the cause of Texas, and Columbus was the rendezvous of all troops from this vicinity which went to the aid of Texas. After achieving her independence Texas granted to each of the heroes, or their heirs, of her revolutionary struggles, lands aggregating about 4,000 acres. Mr. Thomas' father-in-law moved to Texas in 1872, and in going to Texas to visit him parties here would employ him to look up their lands there, and parties there would employ him to look up the heirs in Georgia, thus getting into the Texas practice. Previous to the late civil strife our city was surrounded by suburban homes, comprising some fifteen or twenty acres each, with beautiful grounds and handsome residences. We give the picture on page 40 of one of those typical ante-bellum Southern homes, the birth-place and present residence of Grigsby E. Thomas, Jr. In 1882 Mr. Thomas, desiring to give everyone an opportunity to secure a portion of these homes, conceived the idea of sub-dividing them into lots and extending the streets of the city through them. In December, 1882, he offered for sale at auction these fifteen acres on Rose Hill, sub-divided into forty-five lots, and to the surprise of everyone the forty-five lots brought about $15,000, where the fifteen acres as a whole would not have sold for $5,000. This broke the ice, and suburban property increased in value from 200 to 500 per cent. Then followed the extension of our city limits and the taking in of the annex, which today adds 5,000 or 6,000 to the population of our city. Mr. Thomas has built two handsome residences on the terrace just in rear of his old house, and parties who purchased at his sale have also built several other handsome residences on the old Thomas homestead on Rose Hill. This old homestead is one of the landmarks of our city, being built in 1837 by the late Judge Thomas, and is today in perfect preservation. This place was selected on account of its situation, on the West brow of Rose Hill, one hundred feet above the city, and commands a view of four miles down the river and two miles up it, including the North Highlands, with Girard, Phenix City and the Alabama hills on the West. To get a view of Columbus and surroundings go to head of Robinson avenue on the Thomas survey and you will get it. To none more than Mr. Thomas is the growth of our city due, more especially the suburbs. Every dollar that he has to spare he spends in buying or beautifying some suburban home or other good enterprise looking to the development of our section. There are those who have invested their money, at the suggestion of Mr. Thomas, in city or suburban property, and have realized great returns from their investment. He loves his native soil and believes in her future greatness. He says in ten years Columbus will have a population of 100,000, extending from Clapp's Factory on the North to Bull Creek on the East.

T. J. DUDLEY & SONS—Manufacturers of Doors, Sash and Blinds, Rough and Dressed Lumber, Opposite Union Depot.

Columbus can well congratulate herself on the number of her manufacturing industries; that manufacturing interests is one of the proudest plumes of her civic wreath, as it is on industrial enterprises of this character that she must rely for her future growth and greatness. Live, go ahead, intelligent industry in the future, taking the place of the unskilled negro labor, will not only add to her wealth and future importance, but will exert a controlling influence on politics and social standing, by imparting the dignity of a genuine manhood to both, and placing her in a fair competitive relation with the large manufacturing cities of the North and West.

A proper consideration of the claims of T. J. Dudley & Sons sash, door and blind factory, render these thoughts peculiarly appropriate.

Mr. T. J. Dudley was born in Hancock county, Ga., near Sparta. He came here in 1831 when quite young. He began the study of the lumber business twenty-six years ago, and in 1872 built the proper buildings; in 1882 was burned out, but afterward rebuilt the present plant. Several years ago he associated with him A. T. Dudley and Frank J. Dudley, his sons, who were then just out of school to enter upon their business career, which acquisitions formed the present style of the firm of T. J. Dudley & Sons.

These young members have proven to be "chips from the old block." They have taken the reins of the business in hand and familiarized themselves with every department of the business, handling it with the skill of old veterans, being quick, active and energetic, and to-day are classed among the most progressive business men of Columbus. Since their connection with the firm there have been added two departments, viz: contracting and building, and the manufacture of sash, doors and blinds, both of which have been made important departments. That of the sash, doors and blinds has been extended, until now they are selling this product into the States of Georgia, Alabama and Florida. Their work is second to none and their prices on material are such as to come in competition with any other manufacturer from any market.

Their grounds are 147x438 feet, and covered with buildings and machinery. Four boilers are used having 125 horse power. On the grounds is a dry kiln 24x100 feet with a capacity for drying 75,000 feet of lumber per week.

Eighty hands are given employment by this firm, which brings the monthly pay roll up to $2,500.

In the establishment of Dudley & Sons are to be found a complete stock of lime, laths, shingles, mantels, builders' hardware and rough and dressed lumber, in fact it is one of the prominent institutions of the city, and conduces in a marked degree to the furthering of the interests of the city and the general mercantile welfare, increasing every year its sphere of usefulness as well as augmenting its resources.

J. W. PEASE'S SONS—WHOLESALE AND RETAIL DEALERS IN BOOKS AND STATIONERY, PIANOS AND ORGANS, ART MATERIAL, PICTURE FRAMES, GLASS AND MOULDING, NO. 1140 BROAD STREET.

The Americans are essentially a great reading people, and every year the taste for reading solid literature is growing. The cultivation of this taste is an evidence of advancement in refinement and culture, and we believe the reading nations of the earth are those who excel in business, commerce, science and art. Of all articles of merchandise that a purchaser has to take on the representation of the seller the piano is most decidedly the one, in buying which the purchaser has to take most on faith. Almost every other class of goods can be tested and examined with more general knowledge of their material, construction, durability and ability to perform what is promised, but a piano is an article that challenges closest scrutiny, and the purchaser, even though he may be an educated musician, unless he is thoroughly familiar with the construction of a piano, can be imposed upon by the many elaborately carved instruments, some of which possess a few good and redeeming features, but which are exceptions to those usually placed on the market. In view of these facts, too much care cannot be exercised in selecting a piano, and as it is usually bought but once in a lifetime, one cannot afford to experiment, but should secure an instrument that will be truly a "thing of beauty and a joy forever." The business house of J. W. Pease's Sons includes in its several departments, books and stationery, pianos and organs, and art goods of all kinds. It was established by Mr. J. W. Pease, father of the present proprietors, in 1845, and was successfully conducted by him until 1890 when his sons, William C. and J. Norman Pease, succeeded to the business. Commenced with medium capital, the increase has been commensurate with the growth of the city, and to attend to the large business requires the services of two male and one female employee, in addition to the proprietors, who give personal attention to the trade. The store-room occupied is 25x125 feet in size, and it is admirably adapted to the requirements of the business. As this house does both a wholesale and retail business in books and stationery, all articles coming under this distinctive term are to be found in the stock, enabling small dealers to purchase in any quantity to suit, and the lawyer, physician or reader for pastime to obtain single volumes on any subject they may wish. The house deals in books of every description, from the most solid, scientific and erudite works down to the light literature of the day, offering books suited to minds of all calibers and inclinations. The stock of stationery is the most complete and best selected in the city, always embracing everything desirable, new and costly. Only the best makes of pianos and organs are sold by this house and would-be purchasers can rely upon being furnished with first-class and desirable instruments from this house. In the art department may be obtained art materials of all kinds, picture frames, glass and moulding. A stock of $10,000 average value is carried, and a large trade is supplied throughout Georgia and Alabama, the annual sales reaching $30,000. Mr. Wm. C. Pease was born here in 1856, Mr. J. N. Pease in 1859, and they have long been closely identified with the commercial and industrial growth of Columbus. They have had fifteen years experience in this branch of business, and they can offer advantages to the trade and those desiring anything in this line that make it a most desirable house with which to establish business relations.

W. J. WATT—Wholesale Dealer in Groceries and Plantation Supplies of Every Description, Office No. 1000, Corner Broad and Tenth Streets, Under Rankin House; Warehouse 8 and 9 Ninth Avenue.

There are some houses in this city whose long and steady career, heavy and extensive transactions and solid qualities, make them landmarks in the history of the past, and prime factors in the commerce and prosperity of the present. Of such the house of W. J. Watt is a prominent representative, not alone from the extent of its trade and the force and energy of its management, but also from the fact that for almost a quarter of a century it has wielded, and continues to wield, an influence on the commercial development of Columbus of the broadest and deepest character. In this connection we give a few brief facts with relation to the rise and growth of the house of Mr. Watt, which is replete with interest. Although founded with small capital in October 1868, the business has since largely increased, by honorable business methods and commendable enterprise, until at the present day it must be regarded as one of the most prominent firms engaged in this particular branch of industry in the city. Mr. Watt occupies a three-story building of large dimensions at No. 1000, corner Broad and Tenth streets, where may be found a most complete and comprehensive assortment of groceries and plantation supplies of every description, valued at $15,000 to $25,000. Seven employes find occupation with this house, and such are its relations and magnitude that it is enabled to offer advantages to the trade not duplicated by many and surpassed by none of its cotemporaries. The transactions are general throughout Georgia, Alabama and Florida, and will reach $200,000 per annum. The amount disbursed for employees wages will reach $400 per month, and in every way the business is carried on in a prompt and most orderly manner. Mr. Watt was born in Jones county, July 15, 1825, and came to Columbus in 1868 to engage in his present business. He is so widely and honorably known that it seems superfluous to speak of his many merits. He has met with that business successs which inevitably follows honesty, industry and economy, and his establishment compares most satisfactorily with others of like nature in the South.

M. H. LEE—Dealer in Fine Millinery, 1114 Broad Street.

There is no more important branch of commercial industry than that of millinery. While the grocer and dry goods merchants are important factors in administering to the necessities and demands of the community, there is no one pursuit to which the elegant and presentable appearance of the female portion of society is so much indebted. Nothing pleases the feminine fancy more than to revel among the beauties and styles of loveliness displayed in a first-class millinery establishment, and if anything could make a lovely woman look more lovely it is a tasteful and bewitching millinery adornment, and in the city of Columbus there is no more attractive establishment of this kind than that of M. H. Lee, at No. 1114 Broad street. This enterprise was started in 1860 with a medium capital, and has increased most satisfactorily each succeeding year. The store-room occupied is 35x90 feet in size, and in it is displayed a large and carefully selected stock and assortment of seasonable millinery goods, consisting of ribbons, laces, flowers, feathers, hats, bonnets, trimming silks, velvets, etc., valued at $5,000. One gentleman assists in the business, and from four to six female employes are engaged as the season demands. In all respects the work done here need not fear comparison with that done in any section of the country, and the extensive patronage which the store enjoys is a proof of its popularity. The local transactions through Georgia and Alabama reach $20,000 per annum, and the work of this house is noted for elegance and perfect taste. Mr. M. H. Lee was born in Ireland, but has resided here since 1857. An experience of thirty-eight years in this trade, and the unvarying success of the house since its inception is sufficient guarantee that the demands of this line of business are fully met and patrons served promptly and in a satisfactory manner.

H. F. EVERETT—The Stove Man, 1111 Broad Street.

It is questionable if there is any city in the South surpassing Columbus in natural and acquired advantages as a business centre; certainly none offering comparable inducements for the investment of capital, or a better field for the exercise of enterprise, the assurance having become patent, from her commercial history, that either or both, sagaciously and honorably employed, will return substantial profits. Appreciating these facts, Mr. H. F. Everett decided to embrace the opportunities offered, and in 1878 the firm of Bradford & Everett was established. Mr. Everett has succeeded to the entire business, and he makes no grand display merely for effect, but the stock of stoves, tinware, etc., he keeps on hand are always of the best and of the very latest popular patterns. Mr. Everett is one of those few men who believe in keeping up with the times, and instead of having on hand a large assortment of old-style and inferior goods, he makes it a point to keep the best and most reliable articles the market affords. He has ere this found that the policy thus adopted is the only correct one, and, of course, being free of a large amount of dead capital, he is enabled to place his goods down on a small margin. He sells the New Enterprise stoves, Charter Oak stoves and genuine Iron Witch and Iron King stoves, leading makes, as will be seen. A full line of house-furnishing goods of every description is carried. The stock of stoves and tinware is valued at $7,000, and five employees are engaged, including competent tinners, as one of the departments is that of the manufacture of various kinds of tinware, sheet iron and copper goods. He has provided himself with the necessary appliances for work of this kind, and personally supervises the business. Mr. Everett was born in Columbus November 11, 1843, and has resided here all of his life. Managing his business on legitimate mercantile principles, honorable and liberal in policy, we refer to him with pleasure, and as a duty, as a representative establishment in his line, contributing substantially to the improvement and progress of the city. This is the largest and most extensive house of the kind in this section.

A. J. BETHUNE—Stationery, Fancy Goods and Notions, 21 Tenth Street.

Among the branches of industry in Columbus, there are none probably that will aid more effectually in satisfying the wants of the general public than the varied assortment of useful articles to be found in a well supplied variety store. We are surprised as we enter to find so much that we need, and so much that it seems impossible to do without. Mr. Bethune keeps constantly an immense stock, consisting of stationery, fancy goods and notions of every description, tin, wooden and willow-ware, crockery and glassware, tobaccos, snuffs, and, in fact, everything a person may call for, as it is headquarters for the above named articles. To our readers we commend the variety store of A. J. Bethune for good goods and fair dealings.

PHILIP EIFLER—Dealer in Guns, Pistols, Cartridges, Sporting Goods, etc., 1005 Broad Street.

A prevailing feature of business in this city, and one which early engages the attention of the observer of our commercial and industrial operations, is the conservative enterprise with which it is conducted. There is no lack of enterprise, individual or collective, no scarcity of that spirit of self-confidence which leads men to unite for the general good, each feeling sure of commanding his own share, no want of vigorous push and willing venture into new fields—but neither is there any wild inflation, any chasing after the *ignes fatui* of trade. Among the solid and substantial houses of Columbus is included that of Mr. Philip Eifler, which has had a creditable history and a most prosperous career of more than thirty years. Occupying a salesroom 20x70 feet in size, centrally located, he displays a full and complete assortment of firearms of every description, with ammunition in its various forms and sporting goods of all kinds, including fine fishing tackle, seines and nets. In connection with this line of business he is largely engaged in the manufacture of tents, awnings, etc., which are specially desirable in this climate. The stock carried is valued at $3,000, and a large and lucrative local trade is supplied, the annual business being placed at $20,000. Three assistants are constantly employed and courteous attention is paid to the wants of customers. Mr. Eifler is a German by birth, but has resided in Columbus thirty-one years. He commenced learning his trade in 1843, and with a thorough knowledge of all its requirements, added to the economy and perseverance possessed by all of his nationality, he has been most successful in his business and is one of our most highly respected citizens. The affairs of this house are conducted with enterprise and judgment, and it has earned and enjoys the confidence and patronage of the trade to whose needs it ministers.

DAVID ROTHSCHILD—Manufacturer of Pants and Shirts and Jobber of Gents' Furnishings and Clothing, Wholesale and Retail Dealer in Dry Goods, Shoes, Clothing and Notions, 1245-1247 Broad Street.

Among the men who, in a few years, have taken a prominent place in the commercial world of Columbus, we would call attention to the gentleman whose name heads this sketch. David Rothschild was born in Germany in 1860, and at nineteen years of age he determined to seek fame and fortune in the distant land across the water. In that year he came to America, and four years later to Columbus. He, while yet in his native land, evinced a taste and talent for business, and, turning this to account, decided to take up dry goods and clothing. After a residence of three years in Columbus, he opened his present house in 1886. From the first his success has been phenomenal, even beyond his fondest expectations. His capital was small at the beginning, but what he lacked in cash capital was made up in push, enterprise, and a love of upright dealing, the three characteristics of a successful business man. His capacity is large, and he does a business that runs into large numbers. He employs twelve salesmen, who are gentlemanly

and polite and vie with one another in a desire to please. His wholesale trade covers parts of Georgia and Alabama, while he does a large local trade. He handles the latest styles in clothing and gents' furnishings, hats and caps, dry goods and notions. His stock is most complete, and is being constantly replenished.

JACOB BROWDY—HATS, CAPS, CLOTHING AND FURNISHING GOODS, 1013 BROAD STREET.

In every city there are certain representative houses of a special line of goods, founded upon the experience and enterprise of the proprietors, the completeness of the stock and liberality of the business policy, to which the public turn with a certainty of finding what they want, and that of the best quality. Of the houses engaged in the clothing business in this city it is entirely safe to assert that none are more entitled to the merit accruing from the above mentioned characteristics than that of Mr. Jacob Browdy, located at No. 1013 Broad street. Starting in a small way with limited capital, Mr. Browdy has enlarged his business to its present extent, increasing his stock from time to time, and now carries a full assortment of clothing, hats, caps, fine shoes and furnishing goods, valued at $20,000 to $25,000. A large and lucrative trade has been established in Georgia and Alabama, principally local in character, and the annual sales will reach $40,000. The building occupied is 30x92 feet in size, and three assistants are constantly employed. Mr. Browdy makes a specialty of fine shoes, does a large jobbing trade in hats and makes clothing to order on short notice, satisfaction being guaranteed in every respect. He endeavors to please his patrons, and the large and increasing trade which he has built up shows his success. Mr. Browdy was born in Prussia and came to Columbus nine years ago. He has had twelve years experience in this line, and in his thorough and detailed knowledge of everything pertaining to or contingent upon his business, has few equals. Prompt, reliable and liberal, with an activity and industry that knows no pause, he has made his house a favorite one for those who have once appreciated the advantages to be derived there in prices.

J. W. CARGILL—STAPLE AND FANCY GROCERIES, CORNER FIRST AVENUE AND ELEVENTH STREET.

Ever since the year of 1870 the name of J. W. Cargill has been familiar to the people of Columbus as a grocer, and there is no branch of business which enters so largely into the general make-up of a city's trade as the grocery business. The city of Columbus has her portion of these important establishments, and none are more deserving of notice than the establishment of J. W. Cargill, who started in 1870 with small capital, but what he lacked in capital was made up in enteprise, industry and business integrity, resulting in a good legitimate increase. With Mr. Cargill nothing succeeds like success, and the success of his business has been almost phenomenal. His business career, from clerk to merchant, is one that he may well feel proud of. Mr. Cargill was born in Lawrence district, S. C., and has lived in this city since 1869. His present store, corner of Eleventh street and First avenue, occupies a space 40x75 feet, in which can be found a complete stock of staple and fancy groceries. His business is conducted on a basis of honesty, punctuality and fair dealings, and he is a man of executive ability and enterprise, and his business conduces to the prosperity of the city, as does his goods to the health of the people. Mr. Cargill is a gentleman of high standing, and in all respects is one of the safest and most substantial men in the country, and, with his good judgment and able management, has prudently provided for the necessities of the future. In his line we can only in justice say: No concern is conducted upon higher principles of mercantile honor, none rival in financial solidity, while for upright dealings and fairness to customers it stands without a peer in this great congregation of commerce and manufacture.

E. M. AVERETT—Wholesale Fruits and Vegetables, Telephone No. 216.

With unequaled transportation facilities, penetrating an immense area of demand in every direction, Columbus is unsurpassed as a trade centre by any other inland mart in the South, and few Southern cities possess equal advantages. Recognizing this fact, Mr. Averett established a wholesale fruit and vegetable house here in 1891, and from a moderate beginning has increased his business transactions until now it extends over a large territory, reaching far through the States of Georgia, Alabama and Florida. Mr. Averett occupies two floors, 30x90 feet in size, where he keeps a most desirable stock of apples, oranges, lemons, potatoes, cabbages, onions, turnips, etc., which he is able to sell to wholesale or retail merchants at lowest possible prices, as he receives these goods in car lots. The stock is of several thousand dollars average value, and is sold out and replenished so often that the annual transactions reach from $40,000 to $50,000. Mr. Averett endeavors to keep the finest quality of fruits and vegetables placed on the market, and in every respect this is a leading house in this line. Four employees are required in handling goods, and orders from near or far are filled in the shortest possible time, and to the satisfaction of all parties. Mr. Averett was born in Muscogee county, Ga., in 1841, commenced work in this branch of trade in 1880, and in a twelve years residence here has gained the esteem of our citizens. This adds another testimonial to the list of successful business houses, attesting the great advantages of this city as a centre of trade.

WILEY WYNNE—Wholesale and Retail Tobacconist, 1208 Broad Street.

All persons who are addicted to the use of cigars and tobacco, and who appreciate the delicious flavor of a prime cigar of choice Havana or domestic stock, as well as those who use good tobacco in any of its various manufactured forms, for chewing or smoking, are directly and personally interested in knowing the precise place where such articles may be obtained. It becomes our duty, therefore, to say to the devotees of the "weed" that one of the favorite resorts with good judges in Columbus is the well known establishment forming the subject of this sketch. Here may be found at all times the most reliable and popular brands, either in large or small quantities, at reasonable prices. Mr. Wynne engaged in this business here in 1867 in a small way, and has built up a reputation for straightforward and liberal dealing second to no house in the city. His stock includes fine cigars, tobacco for chewing or smoking, snuff, pipes and a full line of smokers' articles, which will reach $2,500 in value. Two assistants are employed, and the trade, both wholesale and retail, will reach from $7,000 to $8,000 per annum. The store-room occupied is 20x80 feet in size, and in every way will compare favorably with any similar concern in the city. Mr. Wynne was born in Putnam county, Ga., in 1856, of colored parentage, coming to Columbus soon after, where he commenced operations in this line at an early age. He has maintained an enviable name for reliability, enterprise, and all the qualities that go to make the valuable citizen and prosperous business man. This is a store to which we take pleasure in recommending the citizens of Columbus, and to add that Mr. Wynne is justly entitled to the liberal patronage which he has received from all classes of customers.

J. S. HARRISON & BRO.—DEALERS IN BOOTS AND SHOES, 1105 BROAD STREET.

Every line of the retail business found in other large cities, has a strong representation here, both in number of establishments and the character of the stock kept. The parties having control of these important interests are almost universally gentlemen of enterprise and ability, and have a high standing in the commercial world for integrity and business capacity. Among the leading retail boot and shoe houses, that of Messrs. J. S. Harrison & Bro., situated at No. 1105 Broad street deserves mention. Mr. J. S. Harrison started in business for himself six years ago, with limited capital, but like many of our self-made merchants, a quiet perseverance and determination to succeed has placed him, and through him his firm, on the topmost rounds of the ladder of success. This fashionable emporium occupies a building 30x100 feet in size, where is displayed a choice and most desirable stock of boots, shoes, and slippers for men's, women's, youths', misses' and children's wear, of all styles and grades, from the fine and costly hand-made to the coarser qualities, valued at $10,000. This firm handles none but the very best make of goods, and their full and well assorted stock being bought directly from Eastern markets, enables them to compete with any contemporaries in price and style, to the decided advantage of the customers. The trade supplied includes residents of the city and those visiting the city for supplies, and amounts to $25,000 per annum. Several assistants are employed, and the members of the firm give personal attention to the business. Messrs. J. S. and C. H. Harrison are the individual members of the firm, both natives of this city, and a thorough knowledge on the part of both ensures goods that will compare favorably with, if not surpass in quality, those of any house in Georgia, while the liberal and prompt way in which the establishment is conducted bespeaks an unusual share of popularity. Mr. J. S. Harrison began the study of this line of trade about eighteen years ago, clerking for Mr. W. P. Bedell, an old and experienced shoe merchant, and Mr. C. H. Harrison learned the business with Mr. H. Meyers, commencing about fifteen years ago. Mr. J. S. Harrison holds the position of First Lieutenant of the Columbus Guards, with great credit to himself and the company. Much credit is due this firm for the enterprise and ability they have displayed in establishing this branch of industry, and carrying it to its present high and successful position, contributing largely to the reputation which Columbus holds as a center for supplies.

W. E. JOHNSON—SOUTHERN TRAVELER FOR THE KERR THREAD CO.

No pleasanter task falls to the duty of the statistician than that of present- to the world the character and personnel of the commercial men, and of reviewing the results of their enterprise and energy in the busy drama of commercial life. Men who give both impress and impulse to commercial history are not only the "*abstract chroniclers of their day*," but they are the guides of the people in mercantile life, and the heralds of the broad progress that distinguishes American trade. With the growth of commerce, some men have gained prominence, the record of whose business lives teaches lessons of a most salutary character. It teaches what can be accomplished by the development of native ability and innate executive talent, unassisted by the immeasurable benefits derived from mercantile education. These men, as before remarked, occupy the position of guides, which position they have gained by their superior business qualifications and characteristics of sterling integrity, high degree of commercial honor, clear and decisive thought, quick, prompt action, and filling, also when selected, with rare ability the most honorable and responsible stations. With but few exceptions they are self-made men, who have, aided only by their own exertion and energy, fought their way to prominence, and owe solely to their own self-reliance whatever progress they have made in life. In the very front rank of this class, and we but echo public sentiment, we place W. E. Johnson, "traveler for KERRS' SIX-CORD SPOOL COTTON," one of the foremost men and

one of the most active workers in the advancement of commercial interests. Mr. Johnson is a Virginian by birth, and possesses all the gentlemanly attributes for which those of his native State are so well known. He began traveling about three years ago for his present employers, although under some disadvantages he pursued his business industriously, and with the determination of building up a trade that would eventually stand in the front ranks. He worked steadily and bravely on, by degrees making a lasting impression on the existing trade, and of his success it is not necessary for us to make extended comment; like an axiom in mathematics, it is a self-evident fact; the great quantities of KERRS' SIX-CORD COTTON that he places in his territory, which reaches from Chattanooga, Tenn., to Cuba, tell it in more expressive language than can we with pen and paper. Few men in the country of his age can boast so long, continuous and honorable a business career, and but few in any branch have attained so widespread a reputation for uniform courtesy as has Mr. Johnson, (better known to the trade as "Billie, the Hustler.") With the sterling business qualities of Addison C. Hook as Southern Manager, and W. E. Johnson as traveler, the South will continue to be stocked with KERRS' SIX-CORD SPOOL COTTON.

PATTERSON & THOMAS—MANUFACTURING AND WHOLESALE DRUGGISTS, FANCY GOODS, DRUGGISTS SUNDRIES, ETC., ETC., 1127 BROAD STREET.

The importation, manufacture and dispensing of drugs, medicines and chemicals may justly be ranked, at the present day, among the most important and lucrative branches of business; and there are circumstances connected with the progress and present condition of its several departments which are worthy the attention of the mercantile public. The original apothecary, in primitive times, was the practicing physician, who imported his own supply of drugs and dispensed them himself. It has not been many years since the first legitimate druggist was first known in the United States. Bishop, in his "History of American Manufacture," says: "The war of 1812, and the commercial restrictions which preceded it, caused such a scarcity and dearness of chemicals that numbers attempted the preparation of the more prominent articles, and the complete establishment of the manufacturing business dates from that period. Many of these works were undertaken by foreigners, who had learned something of chemical manipulation in German, French and English factories, or by capitalists among our own druggists who made use of foreign skill in getting their works into operation." The druggist entering the field soon relieved the physician from compounding prescriptions, and thus separated the apothecary from the mere shop-keeper, and elevated the business to a professional rank: and, insomuch as the business touches the science of medicine on the one hand and that of chemistry on the other, it may be logically added that he who is best educated—who combines worldly common sense and prudence with scientific skill—is the one destined to be successful in the pursuit of wealth. Our purpose in this work is to refer, in descriptive sketches, to representative houses in every branch, selecting prominent establishments, as is necessary: considering more particularly those whose success has made them conspicuous, and gained for the proprietors positions in the mercantile history of the city, the character of a business man being properly measured by honorable success. The drug trade of this, or any other city, is one of the most important factors in the make-up of commercial interests, and it exercises an influence not out-measured by any other branch.

The establishment of Patterson & Thomas was founded in 1887. This house took a position in the front rank at the beginning, and has held it yearly, increasing their trade in all sections. With regard to so well known a house but little can be said that is not already known of its importance as a mercantile industry, beyond giving the plain facts of this, the largest, drug house in Western Georgia. The extent of their trade, which radiates through parts of Georgia and Alabama, fully attests the success they have achieved, and the high standard of business ability, scientific attainments, integrity and energy, with which they have conducted their business. The premises occupied, at No. 1127 Broad street, are commodious, convenient and attractive. They have a frontage of fifty feet by seventy-five in depth, and three floors. Everything evinces consummate and cultivated taste in all the appointments of this establishment. They carry a complete and comprehensive line of drugs, chemicals, medicines and pharmaceutical preparations and appliances, and a large assortment of such sundries as pertain exclusively to the business, fine grade brushes and combs, tooth brushes, toilet soaps and fancy articles of all kinds. They make a specialty of surgical instruments and appliances, of which they carry a most complete stock. The firm is composed of Messrs. E. M. Patterson and A. P. Thomas. Both are young men of skill, and Mr. Thomas is a scientific and practical druggist of no ordinary ability. In the prescription department of the business they enjoy a high reputation. The most careful attention is given to compounding physicians' prescriptions in an accurate manner, only the purest drugs being used. They are the sole proprietors and manufacturers of Dr. Hood's Eureka Liver Medicine, a remedy having a high reputation, both at home and abroad. The Eureka is entirely vegetable in its composition. It is not a patent medicine put up to cure all diseases, but only those diseases which attend a diseased INACTIVE LIVER, such as headache, loss of appetite, nausea, biliousness, heartburn, vertigo, costiveness, chills and fever, etc. It has many warm endorsers, as will be seen by the following from Dr. N. J. Bussey, President of the Eagle and Phenix Manufacturing Co., of this city: "I have used Hood's Eureka for a number of years in my family, and I consider it a valuable family medicine, and I do not hesitate to say it is all he claims for it."

In addition to the Eureka Liver Medicine, they own and manufacture the following: Hood's Eureka Liver Pills, Gossypedia, the great remedy for suffering females; Dr. A. W. Allen's Celebrated Liniment, the greatest pain destroyer ever discovered. They also manufacture a full line of flavoring extracts, extra pure, and soda syrup and fine German cologne.

Both the partners are young men of high social standing and high business honor, and their establishment is equally an honor to themselves and Columbus.

THE VERNON HOTEL—George A. Riddle, Proprietor, Corner First Avenue and Thirteenth Streets.

There is no more valuable or necessary convenience in a city than a well regulated, comfortable, home-like hostelry. Columbus has a number of hotels, but none more popular, well regulated and comfortable than that which bears the name of the VERNON, located on the corner of First avenue and Thirteenth street. This hotel ranks as the oldest hostelry in the city, and it preserves many curious and interesting associations. The location is an admirable one, in every respect the most desirable and central in the city, close to the business and financial sections, only one block from the post office, and as convenient to

the depots as any in town. It has been the site of a hotel since 1856, when the present magnificent structure was erected by William and Madison Perry, at a cost of $70,000. For many years it was known as the Perry House, the name being changed about four years ago, when the present owner of the building, James A. Lewis, made extensive improvements throughout the whole building, putting in tile floors in the office, etc. In 1885 the house was leased by Mrs. A. E. Riddle & Son, and successfully run until 1892, when Geo. A. Riddle purchased his mother's interest, and since that time has spared neither pains nor expense to render this the most comfortable hotel in the city, and he has succeeded in the most marked degree. The building is a substantial three-story and basement structure, specially designed and constructed to secure plenty of light and ventilation, having wide corridors, immense dining halls and parlors, large and airy bed-rooms, and many arranged en suite with parlor and bed-room connecting. All the modern improvements have been introduced, including electric lights, electric bells and annunciator connecting every room direct with the office. The office is large and airy, and the rotunda is noted as the coolest place in Columbus on a hot summer's day, and is a place where prominent citizens and strangers can be seen every day. The VERNON covers, together with yard, a full half block of ground, and is entirely surrounded by most beautiful shade trees. The bathrooms, washroom, barbar shop and bar are in the basement, the bar being stocked with the finest grades of wines, liquors and cigars, and pool and billiard tables. Mr. Geo. A. Riddle, the present proprietor of the VERNON, is recognized as one of the most genial landlords in the country, and under his watchful supervision a thorough system of organization is enforced. The staff of fifty servants and employees know their duties and perform them. The house is clean and bright, cheerful, quiet and home-like, while the table is supplied with all the delicacies of the season. It has the largest and best equipped kitchen in the city, in charge of a superior *chef*, and competent staff of assistants. The rate, $2 per day, is remarkably moderate, considering the character of table and accommodations. Special rates will be made to troupes or combinations when clubbing rates are desired, also to families desiring board by the month. Mr. Riddle, though a young man, has a wide range of experience, and is a practical business man, successful in all he undertakes, and the hotel is deservedly prosperous under his guidance, while socially he is known and esteemed by the entire community, the VERNON being the recognized headquarters for all the social clubs in the city, where they hold all their parties, balls and germans. We cordially commend the VERNON and its genial boniface to our readers, and bespeak for all who patronize this hotel, the best of treatment.

D. F. WILLCOX & SON—Fire, Marine, Life and Accident Insurance, Telephone No. 7, No. 1149 Broad Street.

In these days of push and progress, when the population and prosperity of the largest cities are increasing at an unheard of rate, the risk of fire and flood are necessarily materally increased, and consequently the guarding against such catastrophe becomes a matter of gravest consideration. Insurance is the only means of remedying such contingencies. Columbus has ample insurance facilities, all the largest and best companies being represented here. The oldest and strongest agency in the State is here in the firm of D. F. Willcox & Son. D. F. Willcox, the senior member of the firm, is a native of Hancock county, Ga., born there over sixty years ago, and coming to Columbus in 1841. He is a pleasant gentleman of the old school, that class of grand old men of whom there are so few left to teach us of a time when chivalry reigned. A. A. Willcox is a young man of superior ability. He graduated from the University of Georgia in 1880, and immediately went into his father's office. The following are among the leading companies that they represent: Hartford Fire Insurance Company, Ætna Insurance Company, North British and Mercantile Insurance Company, Royal Insurance Company, Phœnix Assurance Company, Commercial Union Assurance Company, Orient Insurance Company, Lancashire Insurance Company. They are the agents for the Traveler's Accident Insurance Company, of Hartford. In the Mutual Life Insurance Company, of New York, they have the longest list of members of any agency in Georgia or Alabama. Those wishing to insure in either Fire, Life, or Marine Companies can obtain from them the most reasonable rates and best indemnity.

THIRD NATIONAL BANK—Corner Twelfth and Broad Streets.

It leads. This is the motto of the above bank. Safe, sound and progressive, its success has been phenomenal, and, though to-day only three and a half years old, it leads all the other banks in the city, both in deposits and in the volume of its business. Very much of this, of course, is attributable to the management of the bank, the very strong Board of Directors being one of the main-springs of the bank's success. The courtesy and attention on the part of its employees, and the progressive and energetic action of the officials, all conspire to the success which it has attained in so short a while.

The banking house of this institution is probably one of the handsomest in the South, and not only pleases the eye and carries with it an air of comfort, but in addition to all this, every modern convenience for protection of the business of the bank, and the convenience of its patrons, have been happily blended in the building located as shown at the head of this article, and which to-day is the most conspicuous in the city of Columbus.

Everybody admires success. Capital always prefers to be attached to institutions which lead. There is a seductiveness about success which lets a bank make its own way, after the people have once had confidence instilled, and learned to patronize the institution.

This bank is a regular dividend-paying one, but its Board very conservatively and successfully have adopted the rule of passing the major portion of the profits to the surplus and undivided profit accounts, so as to build the bank up in the estimation of depositors and customers, instead of declaring large dividends to please shareholders. This course has largely strengthened it, and at the same time entirely satisfied those who helped to inaugurate it, and the present price of its stock in the market, and the utter inability to obtain any of it, is the best index of the estimation in which it is held by the public and shareholders.

Organized in 1889 with a capital of $100,000, with a surplus at present of $30,000, its annual transactions will reach many millions of dollars. From the time of its organization to the present day, it has always wielded a controlling influence upon the finances of this section—an influence uniformly of a beneficial character, of course consistent with its financial management. This is one of the institutions of special prominence, from the fact that it has never faltered, and its obligations have been carried out to the letter. The character of the business carried on is of a purely legitimate banking nature, and the policy upon which it has been conducted is amply shown by the following—the first and last—statements of the bank:

FIRST STATEMENT—FEBRUARY 26, 1889.

RESOURCES		LIABILITIES.	
Loans and Discounts..........$	46,788 14	Capital Stock paid in..........$	100,000 00
Over drafts, secured and unsecured	435 45	Undivided Profits............	1,638 65
U. S. Bonds to secure Circulat'n	25,000 00	Nat'nl Bank Notes outstanding	22,500 00
Due from Approved Reserve Agents..................	43,778 38	Individual Deposits subject to Check..................	107,427 46
Due from other National Banks	16,997 38	Due other National Banks.....	2,716 41
Due from State B'ks and B'krs	6,861 49	Due State Banks and Bankers.	2,367 73
Real Estate and Furniture.....	2,634 31		
Current Expenses and Taxes p'd	2,475 02		
Premiums paid...............	7,312 50		
Checks and other Cash items...	225 95		
Bills of other Banks...........	24,500 00		
Fractional Paper Currency, cents and nickels...............	71 63		
Specie......................	8,455 00		
Legal Tender Notes...........	50,000 00		
Redemption Fund with U. S. Treas'r 5% of Circulation..	1,125 00		
Total...............$	236,650 25	Total...............$	236,650 25

The above was the first statement issued. The following statement, issued during the present year, will show the great increase:

LAST STATEMENT—1892.

RESOURCES.		LIABILITIES.	
Loans and Discounts..........$	358,232,54	Capital Stock paid in..........$	100,000 00
Overdrafts, secured and unsecured....................	14,419 40	Surplus Fund................	13,500 00
U. S. Bonds to secure Circulat'n	25,000 00	Undivided Profits............	15,165 86
Due from Approved Reserve Agents..................	76,930 74	Natn'l Bank Notes outstanding	22,500 00
Due from other National Banks	8,515 03	Dividends unpaid.............	93 00
Due from State B'ks and B'krs	3,957 36	Individual Deposits, subject to Check..................	425,159 74
Banking House Furniture and Fixtures................	15,000 00	Demand Cirtificates of Deposit..	221 10
Current Expenses and Taxes p'd	2,080 83	Due other National Banks.....	4,201 48
Premium on U. S. Bonds......	4,000 00	Due State Banks and Bankers.	8,950 53
Checks and other Cash items...	2,359 84		
Bills of other Banks...........	14,330 00		
Fractional Paper Curency, Nickels and Cents............	56 07		
Specie.......................	23,184 90		
Legal Tender Notes...........	40,000 00		
Redemption Fund with U. S. Treas., 5% of Circulation..	1,125 00		
Due from U. S. Treas. other than 5% Fund...........	600 00		
Total...............$	589,791 71	Total...............$	589,791 71

The Third National Bank has correspondents in all of the principal money centres of the United States on which exchange is sold. The building occupied, located as above indicated, is in every way eligible in location and convenient for the conduct of the business. The present officers are: G. Gunby Jordan, President: J. W. Murphy, Cashier; gentlemen too well known in this community to require personal mention or individual assignment. Filling an invaluable place in the monetary system of this city, the Third National Bank exhibits in itself all the advantages that accrue from an enterprising, liberal and discerning policy, a policy that confers benefits upon others, while in the pursuit of legitimate gain.

COLUMBUS Business College AND SCHOOL OF SHORT-HAND.

W. C. HOWEY AND R. W. MASSEY, PRINCIPALS, R. W. MASSEY, BUSINESS MANAGER.

This is an institution which has enjoyed phenominal success and growth. The most practical and modern methods are employed in all its departments, and the courses of study are thorough and practical in every detail. This is essentially a commercial age, and one of the imparative demands of the times is that those who would successfully engage in business should be trained. To meet the increasing popular demand for practical business training, the Columbus Business College was established, and that faith in Columbus as a location for an institution of this kind was well founded, is evidenced by the great success and prosperity which is has enjoyed. Columbus possesses unrivaled advantages, as a city, for the successful up-building of a school of this character, situated as she is, at the head of navigation on the Chattahoochee river, with splendid railroad facilities, and in the centre of a region the most thriving and prosperous in the South. The school is easily accessible to the hundreds of young people in Georgia and adjoining States who appreciate the value of a business education. A familiarity by the Principals, with the workings of the leading business colleges of the United States, has enabled them to formulate superior courses of instruction, embodying all excellencies and excluding all obsolete theories. In fact, no pains have been spared in elevating this college to a plane equal to any in the land. That this has been achieved, all who will examine the curriculum and investigate the practical results attained, may readily satisfy themselves. Endorsements by business men, of a school of practical training, is the best testimony of its efficiency, and this the Columbus Business College has received enthusiastically, both by business men who have secured the services of its graduates, and through the Columbus Board of Trade, which body, on the invitation of the Principals, appointed a committee to investigate the methods, etc., of the school. The committee, consisting of representative business men, after a careful and searching examination, rendered a report highly laudatory of the college, and unqualifiedly commending it to the public. Columbus is to be congratulated on having a college of business training worthy of such high endorsement by practical men of affairs. The curriculum embraces those branches which are most necessary in the preparation for a successful business career. In the Business Course the student receives instructions in book-keeping, banking, penmanship, business arithmetic, commercial law, business and legal forms, and business correspondence. The student is familiarized with all kinds of commercial paper, notes, drafts, checks, mortgages, deeds, etc., and goes through business operations of great variety, so that he becomes fully equipped for the active duties of business life.

The Short-hand Course includes office reporting, general reporting, type-writing, orthography, paragraphing, punctuation, etc. Personal instruction and assistance is given in all departments by instructors who will be found zealous in promoting the wellfare and advancing the interests of the students, taking pleasure in providing them with every means that may contribute to their thoroughness of preparation and rapid advancement.

Tuition rates are reasonable, and from three to four months are required to complete a course, which will be of lifetime benefit. Good family board is procured for students at $12 to $14 per month, which is a much lower rate than can be obtained in other cities, and is a leading point in favor of this school. We bespeak for this worthy institution the patronage and abundant prosperity which it deserves, believing that great numbers of young people throughout this section of the South will avail themselves of its practical training. On application to the Principals, a beautifully illustrated catalogue and circulars will be sent to any address.

WM. MUNDAY—Livery, Feed and Sale Stables, 934, 936 and 938 Broad Street.

When and how the system of hireing horses, for longer or shorter periods originated, it is probably hard now to determine, but to whatever date and cause it is to be attributed, certain it is that the system as it is now carried out is not only one of our greatest modern conveniences, but an absolute necessity. With the growth of our population has increased the demand for livery teams, carriages, etc., and the business has assumed great proportions. Among the several livery establishments in Columbus, the stables conducted by Mr. Wm. Munday deserves especial mention in this work, as being in every way, a representative one, of the best class of such establishments. These stables, situated on 934, 936 and 938 Broad street, are complete in every way, and are arranged in a manner that affords the greatest convenience in every department. This enterprise was started by Mr. Munday twenty-six years ago with no capital, but with his integrity, industry and honesty he has made a marked success, and attained the highest position among similar establishments in the city. The stables are built of brick, and are two stories high—occupying a space of 125 feet front by 150 feet deep, containing seventy-five stalls, to say nothing of the spacious lot in the rear, besides ample accommodation for vehicles of every description. Mr. Munday has in his charge about sixty-four head of horses that he boards, besides the twenty-five he keeps for riding and driving purposes. Single or double teams can always be secured, and special attention is given to supplying carriages for parties, balls, weddings and other occasions. Ten employees are required in the business. The line of vehicles kept on hand are stylish and of the most popular and recent manufacture, and a most satisfactory and lucrative trade is enjoyed throughout the city. Mr. Munday is known for his honesty and straghtforward dealings, and a business man in the fullest and best sense of the term, and his genial disposition and cordial sincerity have made him extremely popular with all. To our readers, whether residents of Columbus or from abroad, we particularly commend this establishment, which, in the style of stock, turnouts and moderation in price, is not eclipsed by any competitor in the Sunny South.

HAMER & EASON—WHOLESALE GROCERS, 1109 BROAD STREET.

An important feature in connection with the progress and prosperity of the business interests of cities are their well-conducted wholesale houses. In a complete and comprehensive work, professing to present in a reliable manner the commercial facilities of a city, the wholesale grocery establishment of Messrs. Hamer & Eason deserves more than a passing notice. These gentlemen established their enterprise September 1, 1891, and it has assumed a prominent position in the trade. The large and commodious building at 1109 Broad street, which is fully occupied by them, is 35x125 feet in size, and a fine display of goods in this line is made, including meat, corn, oats, hay, flour, tobacco, cigars, bagging and ties, soap, soda, potash and canned goods, which are offered to the trade at bottom prices. Five employees are required in handling goods, filling orders and attending to the various departments of the business. The stock is valued at $5,000, and the trade is principally local, including many planters who come from some distance to obtain their supplies of our merchants. The individual members of the firm are Messrs. George W. Hamer and James T. Eason, live business men, who are well-known and popular with our citizens. Mr. Hamer resides on his farm, three and a half miles from the city, situated on the Georgia Midland Railroad, and is fully conversant with the needs and wants of planters in this section. Mr. Eason came here from Russell county, Ala., about twenty miles from Columbus, in December 1890, and has assumed a prominent place in business circles. Liberal, enterprising and energetic, they promote to a large extent the industrial thrift of the community.

REID & LENOIR—PAINTERS, PAPER HANGERS AND DECORATORS, DEALERS IN WALL PAPER, PAINTS AND OILS, PICTURE MOULDING, ETC., 1039 BROAD STREET.

Our purpose in this work is not to over estimate one house at the expense of others. We merely wish to give, by a truthful narration of facts, a representation of the resources of the city. The past few years have witnessed wonderful advancement in the art of both exterior and interior house decorations, and the business men of Columbus have ever been foremost in catering to the fastidious trade which seeks this market as the source of its supplies. The growing taste for interior decorations of the people of all classes of society is a sure indication of culture and refinement. In this connection we call attention of our readers to the firm of Reid & Lenoir, located at No. 1039 Broad street, who as painters, paper hangers and decorators are entitled to a prominent position among our enterprising houses. This firm have been engaged in this business here for two and a half years, and possessing enterprise, ability, a thoroughly comprehensive knowledge of the requirements of the trade, and industrial courage, they have all the necessary elements, backed by ample capital, that win success in any of the active pursuits of life. The premises occupied are 25x100 feet in extent, and a fine stock of wall paper, paints and oils, picture moulding and such articles and materials as are included in this line of business are displayed to great advantage, this being the leading house in this branch of business in Columbus. They give employment to twelve skilled workmen, to whom the highest wages are paid, and the large amount of satisfactory work finished fully testifies to their thorough and detailed knowledge of everything pertaining to or contingent upon this business. Sign and fresco painting are a specialty, and in painting, paper hanging and decorating, this house is the equal of any in this section. Messrs. Alexander Reid and Frank Lenoir are the individual members of the firm, both prompt, reliable and liberal gentlemen, with an activity and industry that knows no pause. They have made their house a favorite one for those who have once appreciated the advantages to be derived there in prices.

THE COLUMBUS SAVINGS BANK.

In every community, especially so in a manufacturing community, there should be at least one strong, solvent and liberal savings institution.

The national sin of America is extravagance. Anything which tends to correct this should always command the good will of all well thinking men. Nothing so quickly transforms a community from a condition of extravagance to one of independence as a Savings Bank, which not only properly cares for the money of the depositors, but pays interest for doing so.

The Columbus Savings Bank, located in the Third National Bank building in this city, is an institution which strongly appeals to the confidence of the entire community, and, with a paid-up capital of $100,000 and $20,000 undivided profits, its solvency is beyond question. The statement published by this institution the 1st of July shows that a large part of its assets is invested in such bonds as State of Georgia and City of Columbus, securities which always command ready cash, no matter what panic may affect the markets, and giving assurance that depositors in this bank, when they call for deposits, will know that the deposit will come.

This bank leads all other savings institutions in the city, doing an active business in the amount of deposits, and has the confidence of this locality in the safety of the rules which govern it.

Attached to the bank is a modern Safe Deposit Vault, with boxes for the use of customers and the public at a nominal rental. An elegant coupon room, comfortable, convenient, and with pleasant surroundings, is an additional attraction which makes this is a favorite bank with investors and the small savers of the community.

This bank has always been foremost in educating the public in habits of economy, and with no stinted hand has at all times generously contributed to the reading public, literature which told not only of the comforts of independence, but showed the way to attain it. One of the most efficient means which the bank has adopted for training the young idea in the proper way, is a nickle-plated auxiliary savings bank, which it very kindly loans to any one feeling economically inclined. This bank is not a toy, but a strong, durable piece of mechanism, which answers its purpose admirably, and as the bank retains the key, when a deposit has once been made in it by the youthful depositor, it cannot be taken out until brought to the Columbus Savings Bank, where the contents are counted in the presence of the owner, and placed to his credit to bear interest.

The President of this institution has had an experience running over twenty years in Savings Banks, and has an intimate acquaintance with that class of depositors throughout this section. The Vice-President, Treasurer, and Assistant Treasurer are all well known business men, who stand deservedly high, and who are intimately acquainted with their duties, and who acceptably perform them to the satisfaction of the depositors of the bank. The Board of Directors embrace a list of strong names selected from the different avocations incident to business of the community, and are: Messrs. H. L. Woodruff, Louis Hamburger, L. H. Chappell, J. D. McPhail, Robert E. Carter, W. E. Bradley, A. C. Prather, W. R. Moore, James A. Lewis, G. Gunby Jordan and J. W. Murphy.

DR. D. A. HOLMES—VETERINARY SURGEON, OFFICES VERNON HOTEL AND HOWARD'S LIVERY STABLE.

Although Dr. Holmes is a recent arrival in Columbus, his fame as a thoroughly practical operator in veterinary dentistry and surgery preceded him, he having been located for several years in the neighboring State of Alabama. As an expert veterinary surgeon he is without a peer in this country. A graduate from one of the best colleges of veterinary surgery in the Union, a deep student, and thoroughly in love with his chosen profession, he is in step with all the progressive theories and practices of the best schools at home and abroad, enabling him to treat upon scientific principles all the diseases of the animal kingdom and on all matters pertaining to horseflesh, likewise canine and bovine diseases, he takes rank with the leading veterinarians in this country.

Dr. Holmes is also well versed in the training of horses, having spent a number of years of his life on the plains among wild and untamed horses. He made a deep study of the horse in his wild state. He can train the most vicious kicker to be as docile, enduring and gentle as a dog. He can break the wildest horse from any and all bad habits. The writer had the pleasure of seeing the Doctor enter the stall of a regular "man eater," and in ten minutes' time the animal was following him all around the lot. A great many persons imagine that a trainer has some mesmeric or magic power over the animal that no one else possesses, while others suppose them to use some drug or opiate; not so, it is only the application of a principle, and if you work upon proper principles and make no mistake in your work, you will get a proper result. If you employ a principle that will gentle the wild animal, a continuation of the same principle will certainly keep him gentle afterwards. The Doctor can explain to you the principle and mode of application in an incredibly short time. Dr. Holmes is among the best exemplars of his profession. He is a native of Texas, bringing with him that irrepressible vim and peerless spirit characteristic of that section. He is a gentleman of superior business qualities, high standing and good judgment, always conducting his transactions in the legitimate channels of honorable business, liberal in his policy, he has achieved success and gained the esteem and confidence of all who know him.

L. A. SCARBROUGH—Dealer in Groceries and General Merchandise, 1015 Broad Street, Opposite Rankin House.

There are a number of houses in this city which, without any ostentation or striving for prominence, yet transact a business of unusual magnitude, and employ capital and labor very extensively. Of such, that of L. A. Scarbrough is an excellent example, and is most certainly entitled to recognition in this work. The enterprise under consideration was started in 1888, and at once began doing a thrifty business, each year showing a flattering increase over the former. The books of 1891 show a business of $135,000, proving conclusively that Mr. Scarbrough is a thorough business man of tact and skill in the manipulation of the grocery trade, with which he is so familiar. Mr. Scarbrough began the study of his business sixteen years ago, at which time he came to Columbus from Russell county, Ala., and entered the old grocery house of J. W. Clements as clerk, and, influencing a large trade, proved himself to be a most valuable acquisition to the establishment. He remained at this stand with William Redd (who succeeded J. W. Clements) until four years ago, when he began business for himself. His old customers have stood by him, and numbers of new ones have been added to the list.

The stock embraces a full and complete line of groceries and general merchandise, including tobacco, bagging and ties, etc. Seven employees are required to attend to the immense business of the house, and special attention is given to filling orders from the large planters and merchants of the smaller points in Southern Georgia, Southern Alabama and Florida.

Mr. Scarbrough is agent here for the celebrated Lucy Hinton 11-inch 5's Tobacco, which brand to-day holds a firm grip upon the large trade handling it throughout the South. He also has the agency for two other brands that are very largely sold in this section: they are "Gilt Edge" and "Brigham Young," 11-inch 5's.

The identification of this house with the staple industries of the community for the past four years, and the honorable, liberal policy upon which its business has been uniformly conducted, makes it a representative institution of the city. Cordially commending his house to the trade and the public, and directing attention to the manner in which it is conducted, the amplitude of its resources and facilities, and remarking that, as ranking first among a number of contemporaries, the establishment is of that class which commands the respect, confidence and consideration of the city at large.

R. HOWARD—BOARD AND SALE STABLE, AND GENERAL TRANSFER LINE, EAST SIDE FIRST AVENUE BETWEEN 13TH AND 14TH STREETS.

As a convenience to the general public there are few business enterprises that can compare with the livery and boarding stable system of America. One of the most popular and representative establishments of this character in Columbus is that above mentioned. This enterprise was founded in 1885 by the present proprietor, with but a limited capital, in fact, his main stock in trade was enterprise, perseverance and industry, backed by honesty of purpose. The result has been very gratifying to the owner, as is evidenced by the fact that he now employs in and around his stable about twenty-five men. Mr. Howard made his first start about ten years ago, with one mule and dray, and worked daily himself. From that small beginning he now has the largest transfer business in the city, besides running a number of sprinklers. Mr. Howard is an acknowledged authority upon all affairs concerning the selection, care and requirements of the horse, hence his stable has acquired a very liberal and influential patronage. His stables are spacious and commodious, covering 50x170 feet of ground, thoroughly equipped with every requisite, well ventilated, lighted and improved sanitary conditions. First-class and ample accommodations are provided for 200 head of horses, and every care and attention is given to those entrusted to him by experienced grooms and stablemen, and the provender is of the very best quality and supplied bountifully, while extra vigilance is exerted over all vehicles, harness and equipments. Mr. Howard is also a dealer in horses, and when he gives his guarantee that a horse is sound and safe he means what he says, and for this reason his patronage is derived from among our best classes of people and is steadily increasing. Orders by telephone receive immediate response at all hours, and all transactions are based upon a liberal and satisfactory footing.

J. J. KAUFMAN—WHOLESALE CANDY MANUFACTURER, NO. 1026 BROAD STREET.

The increased manufacture of confectionery within the past few years in this country has far exceeded most co-relative branches of trade. In its present development it has many of the distinctive artistic characteristics of French ingenuity and invention, and the preparations of sugar and gum and pure extracts absorbs large capital and affords a livelihood to many persons. Until a recent date most of the confectionery sold in Columbus, and territory tributary to it, was manufactured in Northern or Eastern cities. Now we have a home institution which will supply the trade with pure goods. So great is the competition in larger cities that the ingenuity and inventive talent of manufacturers is exercised to find some substitute for the costly sugar, flavoring extracts, and essences, and coloring material, and frequently noxious and poisonous substances are resorted to by manufacturers who manufacture for exportation to smaller cities. These poisons, which are generally mineral substances, are much cheaper than genuine extracts. There is, we feel confident in saying, no more careful and conscientious manufacturer of candies in the country than Mr. J. J. Kaufman. He takes the greatest precaution to exclude adulterated and poisonous ingredients, using nothing but pure sugar, genuine fruit extracts and flavoring essences, and no where can there be produced more brilliantly colored or pleasantly flavored, and what is more important, purer confections than Mr. Kaufman's. Not an ounce of terra alba verdigris, mercury, paris green, analine, prussic acid or counterfeit imitations of any kind can be found in his establishment.

This important enterprise was started in 1885, with small capital, and the increase in business has been so marked that to-day it ranks among our foremost institutions. The building occupied is three floors, each 35x90 feet in size, and is admirably fitted up for the manufacture of candy, containing a number of candy machines and various appliances by which the cost of production is materially reduced. The capital invested is placed at $6,000, and a large trade can be supplied at short notice. Four male and one female employes are engaged in the work, at a monthly outlay of $125. The States of Georgia, Alabama and Florida each contribute their quota of trade to this leading enterprise, whose transactions will reach $40,000 per annum.

Mr. Kaufman was born in Columbus in July, 1870, and has spent his life among our citizens, where he is well known and very popular. He is an energetic, active business man, thoroughly conversant with his business, and justly merits the esteem and confidence of the business community and the trade generally.

DRS. SIMS & SIMS—PHYSICIANS AND SURGEONS, FIRST AVENUE AND THIRTEENTH STREET.

As scientific, practical and experienced professional gentlemen, the above-named firm is deserving of special mention. The firm is composed of two brothers, both natives of Georgia, and was started in 1888. Their superior skill as physicians and surgeons soon placed them in the front rank of the profession in this city. The senior member of the firm, Dr. J. Henderson Sims, began the study of medicine under his father, who was a physician of much prominence, in Covington, Ga. After reading in his father's office, he went to Atlanta, Ga., where he took a full collegiate course in the Southern Medical College, and had the honor of Valedictorian of his class in 1881-2. In 1887 he went to New York for the purpose of more fully perfecting himself in the profession he had chosen. He first entered the Post Graduate School of Medicine, which is one of the most popular institutions of the kind in the world, and took a full course of lectures there, also a full course in the Polyclinic School. While taking these courses of lectures Dr. Sims was not idle in the way of obtaining all the information to be acquired by practical work among the hospitals both in New York and Brooklyn, and had the honor of being chosen first assistant to Dr. Andrew Currier, the celebrated gyneacologist, of New York, and also private assistant to Dr. Camnan, the noted and world-famed specialist in chest diseases, thus giving him the very best of practice even while he was attending lectures. He also attended the Clinics at Rosevelt, New York, St. Luke and Mt. Sini Hospitals, thus fitting him to practice with eminent success in any part of the United States.

Dr. E. H. Sims, the junior member of the firm, also began the study of medicine with his father, after which he attended the leading medical colleges and graduated with high honors. He has also had a wide and extended experience in hospital practice in the North and South.

As a firm they stand deservedly high in the estimation of the public as physicians and surgeons of ability and learning, whose opinions on diseases of all kinds is looked upon as authority, they being often called in consultation with the older physicians of the city. Socially they are both gentlemen of refinement, honorable, upright and straightforward in all their dealings, they have attained a position in this community of which they may well be proud.

SEE PAGE 99.

SEE PAGE 104.

BEGINS Oct. 26th. CLOSES Nov. 5th.

CHATTAHOOCHEE VALLEY EXPOSITION,

COLUMBUS, GA.

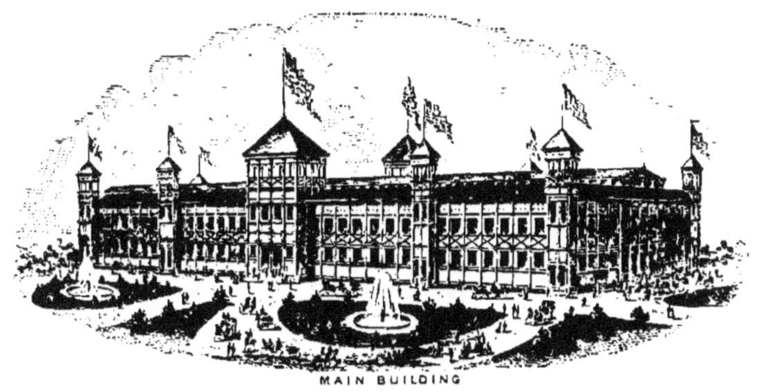

MAIN BUILDING

A Season of Unrivaled Attractions,

MAGNIFICENT RACES

—AND—

LIBERAL PURSES,

PREMIUMS

for County and Individual Exhibits.

A World of Amusements of Every Character.

ONE CENT A MILE ON ALL RAILROADS.

EVERYBODY IS COMING TO COLUMBUS.

SAM'L A. CARTER, Prest.

C. A. ETHREDGE, Sec'y.

www.ingramcontent.com/pod-product-compliance
Lightning Source LLC
Chambersburg PA
CBHW031438280326
41927CB00038B/909

* 9 7 8 3 7 4 3 3 9 5 3 5 0 *